A MAN IS NOT A FINANCIAL PLAN

JOAN BAKER

A MAN IS NOT A FINANCIAL PLAN

INVESTING FOR WEALTH & INDEPENDENCE

ALLEN&UNWIN

First published in 2007

Allen & Unwin
83 Alexander Street
Crows Nest NSW 2065
Australia
Phone: (61 2) 8425 0100
Fax: (61 2) 9906 2218
Email: info@allenandunwin.com
Web: www.allenandunwin.com

National Library of Australia
Cataloguing-in-Publication entry:

Baker, Joan, 1956- .
A man is not a financial plan : investing for wealth and independence.

ISBN 9781741752083 (pbk.).

1. Women - Finance, Personal. 2. Investments. I. Title.

332.02402082

Edited by Dmetri Kakmi
Set in 11.5/14 pt Bembo by Midland Typesetters, Australia
Printed in Australia by McPherson's Printing Group

10 9 8 7 6 5 4 3 2 1

Author's note

I wanted to write a book on wealth for women—a book that spoke to them directly and acknowledged their concerns and the different challenges they face. Sure, there are plenty of books on financial freedom and wealth—I have written/co-written some of them. But as so many women have said to me over the years they find it hard to find themselves in these books. They have to 'read themselves back in'. This book is just for you.

Contents

Introduction ix

Part 1: Getting the life you want

Financial freedom is not for every woman 3
Your financial freedom 6
A man is not a financial plan! 13
A simple plan for wealth and freedom 16

Part 2: Creating wealth through investment

How wealth is created 23
Why income matters 25
How income makes you wealthy 27
You must create a surplus 31
Simple budgeting 34
From mindless to mindful spending 38
Or simply pay yourself first 43
Maximise income 47

Part 3: The principles of investing

It's not luck 53
There are only three investments 56
Buy investments for their yield 61
Markets are emotional 67
Manage your risk 76
You make money when you buy 90
Borrow smartly 100
Time matters 108

Superannuation 121
Getting good advice 128

Part 4: Planning your investment strategy

Does gender make a difference? 139
What's the best investment for you? 142
How much risk can you take? 155
How diversified should you be? 158
How much should you have offshore? 162
Should you invest directly or use managed funds? 166
How should you allocate your investments? 169
Making property investment work 174
Making direct share investment work 181
Big stories—not to be missed! 188

Part 5: Taking action

Doing what it takes 195

Introduction

There's no guarantee that life comes with a man. Even if it does, there's no guarantee that money comes with that man. And even if you get a man who comes with money there's no guarantee that either will stay. At some level we all know this but too many women still rely on men to bring home income, to manage their finances and to invest for the future. We all know that this is not right. We all know that a man is not a financial plan.

Women need to create their own wealth—they need financial plans of their own. Wealth really matters because it determines your choices and options throughout your life. Without money of their own women struggle to have and do and be what they want. Income from work is not enough—the money stops when the work does. Women need to create enough wealth so that some day they have enough money to live comfortably without needing to work.

Women need to plan to grow wealth. It doesn't just happen. High income by itself is not enough to grow wealth: you need to understand how wealth is created. You have to have a plan to create wealth; then you have to work the plan. It is great if you can do this with someone you love but it is a major mistake to rely on a partner to plan for wealth and to carry out that plan.

Don't settle for just getting by. Far too many women live restricted lives, especially as they grow older, because they do not have enough money to have a fuller and more satisfying life. Some of these women have relied on their man for their wealth—but found that he has not been there when he was needed. You can and should be wealthy. The world is full of wealthy people—why shouldn't you be one of them? We live in an era of unprecedented growth and have booming markets worldwide. You need to take advantage of these great times and choose to become wealthy.

Investing isn't hard—it's only primary-school arithmetic. Sure, there's some jargon but that's only some new vocabulary. And creating enough wealth to give you choices for the rest of your life makes learning a few new words and ideas worth the trouble.

Any woman can become wealthy. Not all women will but any woman *can*. Wealth is created through investment and this book will explain how to go about investing. Decide today that you will be a wealthy woman; decide today that you will be self-reliant. Learn to invest and plan to get the life you want. Your man is not your plan—start today to build your own wealth and freedom.

PART 1

GETTING THE LIFE YOU WANT

Financial freedom is not for every woman 3
Your financial freedom 6
A man is not a financial plan! 13
A simple plan for wealth and freedom 16

Financial freedom is not for every woman

This book for women is different. When I wrote *Smart Women, Smart Money* (Allen & Unwin, 2004) my aim was to help women develop smart money habits that would keep their heads above water financially. It was aimed at women who had fairly conventional goals—to manage their money a little better, save money on their mortgage, and protect what they have. Most women do not want much more than this.

Most of my professional work with women has been to show them how to repay debt quickly, and then build a store of wealth through a diversified portfolio containing good solid investments. I believe passionately in the general process of paying off debt and then investing safely. The idea of getting rid of the mortgage and then spreading savings around a range of investments works well. It may not be spectacular, it may not make you rich, but only a few women set out with riches in mind. Most women want to feel safe and secure, perhaps do a bit better than average, but not much more than that. That steady diversified portfolio is right—for most women.

Paying off the mortgage before investing, and then investing in super funds and the like will increase your wealth by around 4–5% per annum. That's fine if your goals are modest. If you follow the usual pattern of repaying debt and then making steady investments you will not go far wrong. If you do this well you will do a bit better than 'all right' and have a nice comfortable lifestyle—just what most women are looking for.

But, as I said, this book is different. *This book is not for most women.* It's for those who want more than just a nice comfortable lifestyle; those who want to be wealthy and achieve financial freedom. Women who want to become wealthy have to do something more than repay debt and find a good super fund. This book is for them; this book is the 'something more' so that you can do a bit better than merely get by.

It's not easy to achieve riches and financial freedom, and it does require some sacrifices. Having said that, anyone can become financially free; there are no prerequisites, like intelligence or a special set of abilities. In my experience, however, only a few will make the commitment that is necessary. You will not be stopped from achieving a high goal by the lack of any particular ability—but you do have to *want* it. You have to want it a lot! More than anything, I have found that it is the desire and the commitment that makes the difference. These so-called 'soft' skills of vision, motivation, determination and attitude are the most important, but the hardest to learn.

The ideas in this book come from nearly twenty years of giving professional advice and from the WealthCoaching clients that I currently have. The main thing I have learnt is that anyone can become financially free, but you have to know what it is you want and you have to want it enough. If you do not want it a lot, you will not be able to do some of the hard stuff that is necessary, nor will you have the 'stickability' to be a good investor. Do not go into this half-heartedly. Either decide to go all out for financial freedom with commitment and energy, or stick with repaying the mortgage and a good solid diversified portfolio with a comfortable lifestyle. The interesting thing about money is that there is no single approach that is right for everyone. We all have different dreams in life (and therefore financial goals), and different strategies need to be employed to meet different goals. If your goal is to move up and above the crowd, read on.

Your financial freedom

If you are reading this book then your ultimate goal is financial freedom. What does it mean to be financially free? It's not just about having enough income to cover your needs. It's not even just about having some savings. Financial freedom is about having enough wealth so that you need not work. You might choose to work for money, but there's a big difference between *choosing* to work and having to. Financial freedom is not something that happens overnight (unless you inherit a lot of money, marry a multimillionaire or pull off a successful bank heist!). In fact, it is likely to take years if not decades of effort. But financial freedom should be your goal, so that some time in the future you will have enough money to live life on your terms and be reliant on no one else for funds.

Think about what that would be like: financial freedom is that happy state where both your money and your time are your own. You have enough money to live the life you want and you no longer need to work to earn it. Time and income are important. The financially free have plenty of both. Many of us have enough of one and not the other.

Where do you stand in all of this?

Take the time to think about it now. Do you have a low income and too little time? Or do you have a low income and lots of time? Some of you might be in the enviable position of having a high income, but too little time. And others might have a high income and lots of time, in which case you have already achieved the objective of this book: financial freedom!

Financially free—having time *and* money

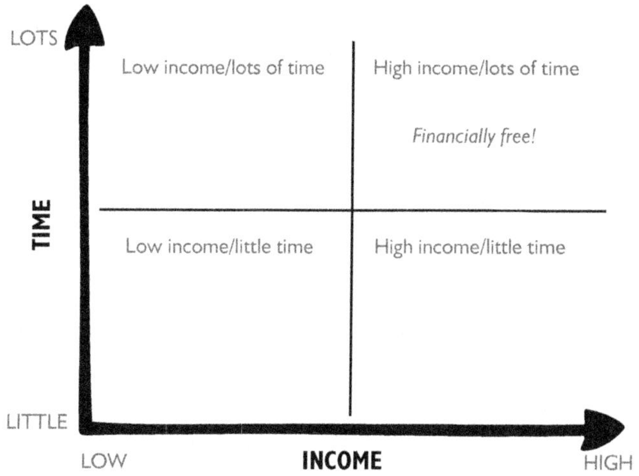

Low income and little time

Some of you may have considered your situation and noted that you have neither lots of income nor lots of time! You may be working hard but not earning very much, or your income may be low owing to the care of children, but you are busier than ever before. Some women may not be earning any income and are reliant on someone else or government benefits for money. Many women with young children are in this position. Even if you are partnered and he is working, income may be barely sufficient. Others may be managing alone after a break-up and trying to stretch a benefit and child support payments to cover household needs. All of these scenarios are normal—we all have periods in our lives where there never seems to be enough time and/or enough money. That's perfectly understandable. However, this ought to be a transitional period, not the end point. You need a plan and a vision so that you do not stay in this position forever. Every woman needs a plan to make sure that sooner or later she has enough money and enough time to live the life that she wants. This is what financial freedom is about. Why shouldn't you have a great life? Why shouldn't you have enough time and money to do at least some of the things you have always wanted to do or be or have?

Low income and lots of time

Some women find themselves with plenty of time but low incomes. An unemployed single woman might be in such a position. This is also a common scenario in later life where a woman is living on a pension. And while these women may not be rushed off their feet caring for small children they often find themselves without the means to do much that is enjoyable with their time. If you are a younger person in this position you need to urgently plan for change. All of us should be making certain that we do not find ourselves in this space as we get older and our options for creating wealth become limited.

High income and little time

Many of you will already earn a good income. You may have a great lifestyle and your money may well cover lots of your wants as well as your needs. However, if you are well paid you probably work quite hard and put in long hours to earn that money. And the salary will stop whenever you do. So while you have plenty of income your time is not your own. Have you stopped to ask yourself how much income you would have if you did not work? Have you thought about how you would live if for some reason you had to stop working? What will you do when you no longer work or circumstances change and you are not so well paid?

Perhaps your high income and living standards are due to the fact that you are partnered to someone who is well paid. Many couples have a high household income and great lifestyle because each of them works. What would happen to your income and lifestyle if you lost your partner's income? This could happen for several reasons: illness, death, divorce, redundancy, and so on. My experience is that women are especially vulnerable to the loss of income through their partner. It can't be a secret to any woman today that nearly half of all first marriages end in divorce and the rate of break-up of other types of relationships is even higher. Women are especially vulnerable if they are relying on men for much of their income as they often find it extremely difficult to replace this income: a woman may have curtailed her career in the interest of her partner's, or she may have chosen to stop work in order to have children, or she may find it very difficult to re-enter the work force at a well-paid level.

Of course, all of the above life events are very difficult for men too, but it is usually easier for them to recover financially because they are generally earning more, haven't taken time out of the work force for family and, in the case of a relationship break-up, are usually less constrained by child care. While there are, no doubt, exceptions to this picture many of you will know women who have had their incomes severely limited in some way or other. So even if you are a high income earner, you need to give some thought to how secure that income is.

High income and lots of time

This is the ideal place to be in, and the younger you can achieve it the better. This is financial freedom. You have enough money to live life as you want to and you do not have to spend all of your time working for it. Unless your chosen lifestyle is an extremely cheap one, this usually means that you have plenty of passive income—income you do not have to earn. Passive income is money that your wealth provides, such as rentals from property you own, dividends from shares, interest from deposits or income from a family business or a trust. Being in this space does not necessarily mean that you no longer work. Many financially free women work. But they work because they want to, not because they have to. Work can be very enjoyable and liberating, especially when it's your choice and particularly when you are not depending on that income to meet your everyday needs. And, of course, a woman who is financially free also has the choice of working on a voluntary basis, such as for the community or a not-for-profit organisation.

Your financial picture

Think about where you sit in the financial-freedom picture. Consider what will happen if you do nothing about your finances. And without wishing to scare you, if you are depending on a man for your current income and future financial freedom, think again. You may be very lucky; then again you may not. Even the most handsome of princes have been known to turn back into frogs! It's this book's philosophy that your future financial security and freedom is far too important to be left to any man.

Whether you are happily partnered or not, you need a plan to make sure that some day you will be financially independent. And a man is not a substitute for your financial plan. Many of you will be happily partnered. Many of you will already have an enviably good income and lifestyle with a partner. You may be lucky enough to have a stable relationship with a generous and supportive man. All such women have been lucky enough to find a prince among princes. Many others will be hoping to find a life partner. However, it is neither sensible nor desirable for a woman to count on a man to provide financial freedom. All kinds of things can derail such a plan, and what then will become of your dreams?

There's no guarantee in the first place that money will come with a man. Many of you will earn more than the men in your life. Many men will also prove irresponsible with money in a variety of ways—indulgent spending, lots of toys, gambling, reckless investments or business decisions. Money can go with a man too!

With or without a man in your life you need a plan for independence, security and financial freedom.

A man is not a financial plan!

Too many women still rely on men for income. Many do not earn any income at all, or only a small amount. These women rely on a man to provide both now and for the future. Others are in dual career families and may earn a good income today but are without a plan for the future. What will happen when the income stops? Even if you are partnered you cannot rely on a man to plan for your financial freedom. In my WealthCoaching work I have met several couples where little or no financial planning has been done throughout the relationship. In many cases she has deferred to him, choosing to believe that it's his business or his career. And for varying reasons he may have taken no action. He may be more interested in his profession than in securing the family's financial future. Many of the couples have come to see me at the woman's urging as the man may be indifferent or even reluctant.

Once I start to talk to women about what they really want in their lives and about charting a path to make sure that they get it, it's amazing how involved and energised they become. Often women initiate the process because they are more realistic about what can go wrong in their lives. Death, disease, divorce or redundancy can have devastating effects on your finances, especially if you are not well prepared.

But it's even more important to have a financial plan in order to make sure that the good things in life happen, to manage the upside as well as the down. Your financial freedom is far too important to leave to chance. You need a plan of your own! This is an area where you may have to take the lead. Some men will be delighted that you have initiated this, while others will need to be convinced it was their own idea. However you manage it, don't delay—you can't afford to waste another year.

Many single women earn well and can provide a good lifestyle. I meet many who are high achievers with a healthy income. Their consumption levels, however, are usually very high and often they have no wealth reserves. They are not thinking ahead and simply concentrate on their job and having a great social life. But sooner or later the income will stop. What then? Unless you plan well for later life your choices will be very limited. Life will be very restricted if you depend on the state for support and income during retirement.

Some singles are still hoping to meet the man of their dreams and perhaps expecting that he will provide for the future. This is not a good strategy: your prince may never come. And even if he does, he may not have accumulated wealth and may have no plan for financial freedom. Relationships can also be very complicated. Many women who are partnered find themselves in blended families. These can be challenging to sort out from a financial point of view, particularly if you too have children from a former relationship. You risk being in financial conflict with stepchildren in the future—not a nice prospect for any woman who finds herself alone.

Statistically, many women will end up alone. Separation from a partner can really affect your finances. While there's no guarantee that money will come with a man, it's very likely to disappear with one! Partners and husbands may leave but you need to make sure that they do not leave you without the means to take care of yourself. Older women are especially vulnerable. Most women over sixty-five live on their own. And women alone are likely to be poor. It is very difficult to earn income or create wealth if you leave it too late. Your money, security, independence and future choices are too important to neglect. You wouldn't neglect to take care of your skin or forget to plan for regular smears and mammograms, so why would you fail to plan for your money?

A simple plan for wealth and freedom

In many ways women have never had it so good. Over the last decades many of the barriers women faced in getting an education or entering the work force have been removed. Girls do better at school at almost every level, more young women than men enter university, and women are outperforming males on many criteria. Women still struggle to earn as much as men but we have equal pay legislation and the right to equal treatment under the law, if not always in practice. Many women have achieved very high levels of success in business, in the public sector and in many other areas of life. If there was ever a time in history to be born female in this part of the world it is now.

More women than ever are entering the work force. Collectively we earn a huge amount of money. It's easy to underrate the power that comes with the ability to earn an income and forget that women in previous generations either could not or were not allowed to earn money. We take for granted many of the rights and freedoms that recent generations of women have acquired and fail to recognise how many of these rights are maintained and secured by the ability to earn and keep money. You only have to look at the lives of women in some parts of the world to see what little choice a woman has when she has no economic opportunity or financial security.

So what are we doing with all of this opportunity and education and money? Well, women are generally very good at managing day-to-day finances and in many families they take the lead in managing the family accounts; however, despite the advances and achievements, many women end up poor in their middle years or later life, even though they have worked hard and behaved responsibly. One of the reasons for this is that women are still inclined to rely on a man rather than on themselves for long-term financial security.

In many households women take care of all of the day-to-day money and their partners look after the rest, like investments, superannuation and tax. It's easy to see how this happens. Sometimes it's because the man is older when they get together and has established patterns in his handling of money. Often it's because women choose to stay at home for family reasons and end up taking care of all the daily money—children's expenses, homemaking, child care, clothing, holiday spending and so on. All of these are very important, of course, and have a great impact on how we live. But the focus of these concerns is immediate and short term—getting through this day, this week, this month. Women usually work hard to meet the needs and wants of everyone in the family with only the occasional treat for themselves. Even single women may focus only on how they live in the shorter term, managing living expenses and perhaps planning for holidays and lifestyle purchases.

The problem with this approach is that we are likely to overlook the bigger financial questions. Whether or not you have a man in your life, you need a plan for financial freedom.

A financial plan sets a strategy to make you financially free. The plan needs to take account of what you want in your life and to arrange your finances so that you get to live that life. A good financial plan will take account of where you are financially and what you need to do to achieve the lifestyle you want in the future. It will almost always mean that you have to make some changes about what you do with money. For instance, you may need to earn more income or spend less; you may need to learn to invest or you may need to exit some poor investments already made.

To plan well, we need to ask ourselves about the things that matter for our future wellbeing:

- Are we just getting by or is our situation improving?
- How well will we be able to live in the future?
- Will we ever be able to stop working?
- What choices will we have in the future?
- Will we be able to take care of our future needs?

Wouldn't you like to know that your future needs, and some of your wants, are taken care of? This is what a financial plan is about.

It's a simple plan

The best plans are simple. When it comes to creating wealth there are three critical steps:

1 **Deciding that you will be wealthy in the future.** This seems easy to say but it is in fact a major decision. It's a life-changing step because it means that you have made a choice: you have chosen wealth. Many other things may have to change to make this happen so you need to be certain that you want wealth and financial freedom—and you need to be sure that you are willing to do what it takes to make that happen. I hope I have convinced you that this is a commitment that you should make—if so, you have already achieved the first and most vital step. Written commitments are best: I recommend that you write down a promise to yourself that you will create the wealth you want. You can take this step right now.

2 **Learning what you need to know about creating wealth.** The second part of your plan is to learn, so the rest of this book is devoted to helping you understand how wealth is created. You have to invest in order to create enough wealth for financial independence and freedom from the need to work. Learning to invest is not nearly as difficult as many women believe. Like many other topics it's mostly jargon—that's what men do with things that interest them like cars, sport, business and so on. This book explains the basic principles that you need to understand and I think you'll agree that they are common sense. I have kept the jargon to a minimum and focussed on giving you all the understanding you need to become a successful investor.

3 **Taking the necessary action.** Knowledge and skill about investing and creating wealth are necessary but are

not enough: you have to actually put what you learn into practice. For example, it is easy to learn how to create a surplus so that you have money to invest. However it can take a lot of determination to change some of your habits so that this money ends up invested rather than spent! Consuming every dollar of income is much easier than finding the motivation to put it aside for investment. Learning to say 'no' to others (such as children who are demanding treats) so that you can follow your plan to invest takes lots of determination. Many women think that finance and investment are all about difficult technical terms and advanced mathematics. Not so—you learned all of the maths you will need at primary school. The really hard part of becoming a successful investor and creating wealth is changing your attitude to how you deal with money and developing new habits that will make you richer rather than poorer. Like most new behaviours, it's hardest at the start; after a while you will feel so good about the wealth you are accumulating that investing will be one of your favourite activities. I can only encourage you to move into action: *you* will have to act.

PART 2

CREATING WEALTH THROUGH INVESTMENT

How wealth is created 23
Why income matters 25
How income makes you wealthy 27
You must create a surplus 31
Simple budgeting 34
From mindless to mindful spending 38
Or simply pay yourself first 43
Maximise income 47

How wealth is created

If you really want to become financially free you first need to understand how wealth works. Many women approach wealth as if it is a matter of luck. Others think that you have to have a lot of money to make money. Neither is true: wealth is created following some basic rules that you need to understand so that you can make use of them, and have some fun doing it!

Being wealthy is not about having a lot of income. Instead it is about having a lot of *capital*. The ultimate aim is to have lots of income, but this has to be *passive* income, i.e. income that you get without having to work. Passive income can only come from capital, and so you have to grow your capital (your wealth) so that you can get plenty of passive income. Capitalism is the name of the game.

This sounds simple enough; however, women confuse having high income with being rich. Women who have high income, especially when it is from a job, give every appearance of being rich, but they may have no wealth. I have encountered many women, both single and partnered, who had very high incomes but who owned almost nothing. In other words, they took their high salaries and consumed them rather than using them to acquire assets that would give them further income and make them wealthier.

Being wealthy is about having capital, that is, owning assets such as property, shares and deposits that will give you passive income. It is passive income (that you do not have to work for) that allows you to live the life of your dreams. Then you are free to spend your time on what is important to you, and you have enough income to do so. Your time is your own and you have the income you need.

Having lots of capital is the final objective. Remember, capitalism is the name of the game. You have to be an owner: an owner of the right things; however, it is what you do with your income during the time that you are trying to become financially free that is important. A lot of women manage to get high incomes from their businesses or investment activities; nevertheless, because of how they use this income, some do not become wealthy.

- What capital do you have, e.g. a home, investments in funds, deposits in the bank, rental property, shares, etc.
- Is your capital base growing?
- Is it growing fast enough to give you enough income some time in the future?

Why income matters

Income has four important uses:

- **Consumption.** You have to live. A proportion of your income will have to be spent on groceries, transport, utilities, etc.
- **Reinvestment.** If you retain income (i.e. do not spend it) it is added to your capital (wealth) and will grow. When income is invested in good assets it will compound at a good rate and create even more wealth.
- **It pays for borrowings.** Nearly everyone who becomes financially free gears up the capital that they have by borrowing. (More in the 'Borrow smartly' chapter, page 100.) Borrowing reduces the amount of disposable income that you have (because you have to pay interest), but increases the amount of your capital (because by borrowing you can invest in more assets).
- **Setting capital value.** The income that you get from your assets values those assets. Regardless of whether it is a business, shares or property, the value is set by the amount of income that comes off them; therefore, increase the amount of income from your investment assets (shares, property investments, etc.) and you increase their value. For example, if you can increase the rent that you get from a property that you own, the increase not only raises your income but also makes the property more valuable.

- Consider how you view wealth and income. Have you been confusing the two?
- Do you see income as a means to increasing wealth, rather than wealth in itself?
- Are you focussed on increasing your wealth?
- How will you use your income to grow your wealth?
- Do you value your income highly enough?

How income makes you wealthy

Although having a lot of income is not in itself being rich, income is critical to becoming wealthier and, ultimately, financially free. To become wealthy you must generate as much income as you can from work or from investments you have, and then use this income wisely and well.

When financially astute women have a good year with their business and the annual profit increases; when they manage to increase the rents on their properties; when the companies that they are invested in increase their earnings and dividends, they are delighted and happy, and they celebrate. In all of these things, their income has increased and that is very good news.

However, the increased income is not good news by itself. Sure, the extra income is useful—it could be taken out and spent. But few women who are serious about becoming financially free would care for that. The increased income is not terribly important in itself. Rather it is what the extra income can do for you that is important.

In fact, it is the attitude towards increased income that distinguishes the successful from the unsuccessful. The unsuccessful are likely to look at the extra income and start to think what they can do with it: another overseas holiday, a shopping expedition, increase the mortgage on the house to build a swimming pool.

Those who are determined to be successful investors view the extra income quite differently. Instead of thinking about what they can do with this extra income, they think about what the extra income can do for them. Instead of thinking about the 'fun' that they can have with the additional money, women who know how to become wealthy are thinking about the effect on their financial positions and the opportunities that increased income has brought about.

This difference in attitude towards income is the divide between those who will become wealthy and free, and those who will not. Those who will not achieve financial freedom think only of consumption.

Those who will achieve financial freedom think of their income like this:

- **Extra income means that their assets will have a higher value.** All investment assets are valued by their income, for example the family business is valued by the profits it makes; property investments by the rent, and shares by their earnings (in much the same way as the family business). Therefore, someone who owns a small commercial property might be able to increase the rent by $5000 per annum. This person celebrates the extra rent not because of the income itself and its spending power but because the value of the property will be greater (perhaps by as much as $50000). The extra rent (or business profits) increases the value of the asset because someone would agree to pay more for them to get the higher income. The extra income means that you have become richer (you have more capital). This additional capital growth is often worth several times the additional income that was generated.

- **The extra income can be used to borrow more.** Not only will you have higher capital values to use as security but you will also have more income to fund borrowings. The ability to borrow more means that you can dramatically increase the total amount that you have invested. This in turn will generate even more income for you, spinning a virtuous circle of wealth even faster. (More on borrowing later.)

The virtuous circle of wealth

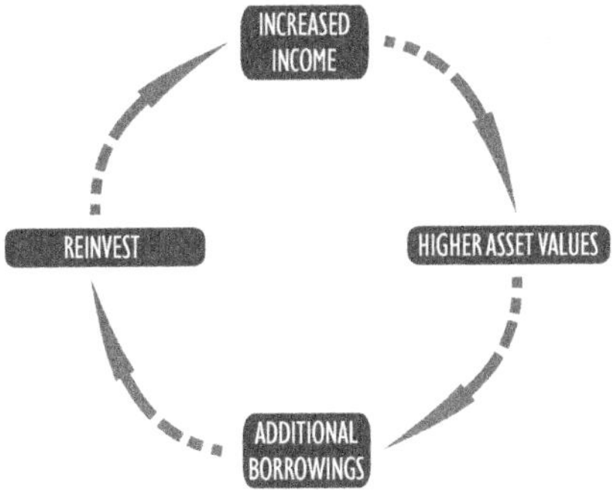

This allows you to compound your good investment choices—you can take any increase in income and use it for reinvestment into more assets. You don't even have to receive the money in order to use an increase in income to borrow more. Lenders will look at the greater value of your existing assets and see them as enough security for further loans. Income itself is important in driving up the value of your investments. It is also important because it allows you to gear your investments further, thus accelerating your creation of wealth.

- What have you been doing with your income? Is there any surplus or are you consuming it all?
- If there is a surplus, where have you been putting it?

You must create a surplus

Investing to grow your wealth is all about creating a surplus. No matter how much or little income you have you will need to avoid consuming all of it. The amount left, your surplus, needs to be put to work to create more wealth. This will be especially true for individuals who have high income and little time.

It's a simple equation:

Surplus = Income – Consumption

Creating a surplus

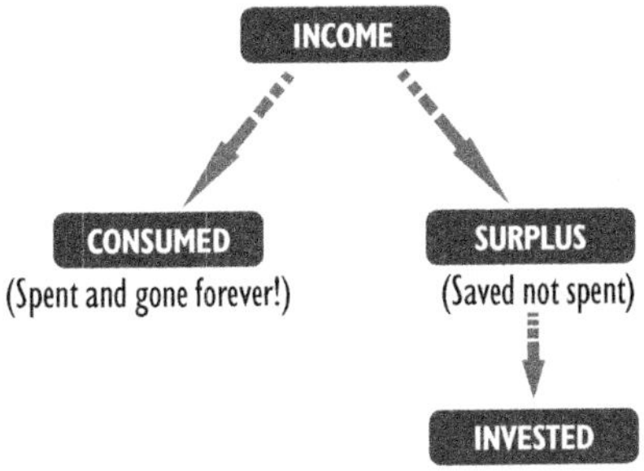

This is very easy to grasp at an intellectual level but it is where the hard work is for most women because it usually means that habits and lifestyle have to change. And other people around you—friends and family—may object to these changes.

Like all simple equations you can play with different variables.

If you want more surplus you can either:

1 lower your consumption, or
2 increase your income, or
3 both!

This is where you will find it very useful to start to work to a money plan, a budget. Women get very strange when the word 'budget' is mentioned. It has connotations of meanness and misery. In my experience, it is helpful to think of it like a business proposal: not as a way to scrimp and scrape, but rather as a way to plan income and expenditure for a period of time. Remember that the choices are yours—it's your money! But unless you create a reasonably sized surplus you will have a very slow path to wealth.

You will need a stake to begin your investment. Unless you are releasing capital from your home that start-up money will have to come from income. All this means that you will need to manage income and consumption very closely. You really need a budget. This should be based on whatever time period is most convenient for you in terms of income (weekly, fortnightly, monthly). It should show your expected income for each period and your planned consumption.

Many women find that once they are motivated, they can consume less and reduce the amount of money they spend. Don't make your budget too strict. If you do, you are unlikely to keep to it. See it like dieting. If you starve yourself, sooner or later you will attack the chocolate biscuits and eat the whole packet. You want a reasonable budget that you can live with and which will avoid big blow-outs.

- Consider what you can do to create or increase your surplus. Remember, it's what is left that counts.

Simple budgeting

You may feel very negative about the idea of budgeting. However, hold on to the bigger goal which is about releasing 'wasted' money so that you can invest it. Every dollar you don't consume can be put to work in wealth creation. So the idea of this budget is not about penny-pinching—after all, it's your money and you can spend it as you please. Rather you should establish a figure for consumption you can happily live with so that you can take every remaining dollar away for investment. How do you do this?

The first part of any budget is to look at what income you have coming in. This could come from a number of sources:

- your job
- your partner's income
- income from any investments you already have, like rentals or dividends
- income from a trust.

Add up all of the income that you are receiving. When you are sure that you have all of your income, you need to allocate it as follows:

- some for consumption
- some for investment.

Now is the time to sit down and discuss what you will agree to consume from now on. You will need to talk about all of the categories—the fixed expenses such as housing, transport and groceries, and the discretionary ones such as entertainment, holidays and hobbies. This will take a lot of work and discussion, especially if you have a partner and/or family, and particularly if you have never worked to a budget before.

You may need to monitor your spending for a while to see exactly what gets spent now. That's easy in some budget areas as you will have utilities bills or cheque butts or credit card statements to refer to. It can be much harder in the areas where you usually pay with cash, or with smaller items that you are inclined to ignore—takeaways, drinks after work, additional spending at the garage when you fill up. Many of the women I have worked with say it took them weeks to get a handle on what they spent in each area. Mostly they report being shocked at the amounts that are slipping through unnoticed! So don't be discouraged in the initial stages. Stay motivated and focussed.

I have no interest in admonishing you to turn down the thermostat, to limit shower times, or to encourage you to avoid takeaways, to walk to work, to grow your own vegetables or offering any other money-saving strategies. This budgeting exercise is about *you* deciding:

1 what must be spent on necessities
2 what you'll spend on leisure, holidays, entertainment
3 what surplus you'll be able to invest.

A key part of any woman's plan for investment is a budget. This is a negative sounding word with connotations of scrimping and saving, and living a frugal life. Well, it does not have to be that bad, but there is a price to be paid for financial freedom, and a reduction of consumption is often a part of that price. Some of my clients call it the 'B' word. But all that a budget does is help you spend in line with your values, spending on what matters to you and not spending on things that are of low value to you. This allows you to make your spending much more *value-able.*

- If you have not already done so, start a draft budget. There are several websites that provide useful categories to budget under. The main value of this is that you will not leave out items that occur infrequently, e.g. rates, car registration, back-to-school expenses, etc. The best site I have seen is www.sorted.org.nz. Almost all major banks provide some kind of budgeting tool online.
- Decide on a total amount that you will spend per year, e.g. $30 000 after tax. What you spend this money on is irrelevant to your wealth creation. All that really matters is that there is a surplus that can be used to grow your wealth. So you will need to choose a consumption amount that allows enough surplus for investment so that you can create enough wealth in the time frame you have chosen.

Clients often ask what they should be aiming for when doing their budget. It all depends on your circumstances. However, a useful rule of thumb is to work hard to live on 80% of your income. This allows 10% for saving and up to 10% for the indulgent and unexpected events in your life, such as house repairs, or urgent dental work.

The budgeting process and then living to that budget is an important part of your plan for financial freedom. This is especially true for those starting off. Making those first few steps, developing a little bit of wealth to get things going, is the greatest hurdle. The first $10 000 will be harder than the next; the first $100 000 will be harder than the second, and so on. They say the first $1 000 000 is also the hardest!

If you are starting with next to nothing, your first investments can only really come from increased income and/or reduced consumption. If you are starting with a little but not very much, reduced consumption will accelerate the process. And don't feel hopeless if you are young and poor and with very little available for surplus—starting early is the best wealth-creating strategy of all. Time is your biggest ally.

This is where the going gets tough. Unless you have a very high income you have to cut your consumption to create a surplus for investment.

From mindless to mindful spending

Managing spending is tough because we have developed a sense of lifestyle entitlement. We now feel that we 'deserve' and have a 'right' to a way of life that not long ago was considered luxurious. There are great and powerful marketing forces telling us to consume more and more. We have become used to living up to, and even living beyond, our means. We consume more of everything than we need, or even really want, in some cases. Most of us are overspending—on food, clothes, holidays and so on. Every business in the land is telling us to spend, spend, spend—and they are backed by huge marketing budgets. Many people spend money they don't have on things they don't need or don't really want just to keep up with or impress a whole lot of people they don't rate or even care about. How silly is that? And keep reminding yourself—you could invest this money to create wealth and make yourself financially free!

You have to resist a lot of this. You have to stop being like 'most women' and cease mindless spending. Largely this spending is about buying things that make you look good in the eyes of others. It is ego-spending, buying things for emotional reasons rather than considering your purchases rationally. To get to financial freedom you have to stop this and be your own person with your own aims. Living below your means, rather than *above* your means, is a key step in releasing money for investment. Every dollar that you spend is a dollar further away from the life you want. Remember, every dollar you don't spend can be put to work for you for twenty-four hours a day, every day. This is the money that will make you wealthy and buy you the life of your dreams.

I tell my clients two things:

1 Before you spend money on something, imagine that you are not spending dollars but GPG shares. GPG is a pet company that has performed extremely well for its shareholders for a decade. At the time of writing the shares are trading at around 238 cents and they look like they still have a future. Don't just take my word for it though: check them out yourself. That means that if you forgo that one-thousand dollar suit you are gaining about 420 GPG shares.

Owning the GPG shares now may be better than owning the suit. But in twenty years time it is *far* better—the suit has gone off to be a duster, but if GPG shares grow at 20% per annum, they will be worth over $38 000. (You should be able to buy a few suits with that!)

I am not saying do not buy the suit (or anything else for that matter). What I am saying is think about the cost not just in dollars today, but dollars in the future. The 'real' cost of your spending is the future value of the dollars you are spending today if they had been invested well instead. There is a very real benefit in doing without something today for a better tomorrow. The ability to delay gratification is a hallmark of successful individuals in all areas of life. The success in this instance is achieving your dream of financial freedom.

Changing your currency to GPG shares (or some other proxy that is meaningful to you) is a good way of recognising the real cost of unnecessary expenditure. That cost is primarily what you can have instead in the future. The only thing that you need to be careful of is that you do not take it too far, and end up mean and miserable and no fun to be around. Which leads us to the second thing.

2 By all means spend money, but make your spending count. Your spending should be 'mindful'. The latest pitch from your favourite department store should not dictate your expenditure. These are companies that you can *own* through the sharemarket, rather than have them own your credit card! Buy quality things that will give you great pleasure. Buy things that you really want and need. Think about your purchases beforehand, rather than buying on impulse because some slick marketing has pushed a product at you.

'Mindful' spending means buying what *you* want, not what everyone else is told that they want. If you get a lot of pleasure from owning a nice car, you might have one. However, do not own a nice car because that is what others expect. Indulge yourself with things that make *you* happy, not which are designed to make you look good. This is a great time to revisit your dream and vision for the future. Many of the things we spend money on do not take us in the direction of our dreams; in fact they take us away. It is much easier to bypass the temptation of 'mindless' expenditure if you are clear about what you *really* want—you can distinguish easily between the 'big things' that matter, and the trivia that does not.

Many women could become financially free just by spending less and investing the remaining money well. I have seen clients 'save' thousands of dollars *per month* from their budgets and develop an impressive investment portfolio within a year! Living below your means becomes a new habit quickly—and a very rewarding one when you see the resulting assets accumulate.

The wealthy women I coach are not mean. They are, in fact, nearly always generous. However, almost all of them are very 'mindful' spenders. They know what they want and they have what they want. But they do not have what they do not want. They are happy to go without if they are not getting the full measure of enjoyment for each dollar spent.

The key bit of knowledge you need here is to understand how a smart budget underpins all of your efforts towards financial freedom. As you play with various options you will develop the skill of allocating income towards the consumption essentials (like power and food) and some valued discretionary items (e.g. entertainment, hobbies, holidays) and away from things that are less important to you. You will find that your attitude to spending will change. You will start to ask whether you want this or that item more than your dream. Over time, you will develop the habits of the wealthy—managing consumption well, ensuring that there is a surplus, and using that surplus to create wealth. Wise women spend as much money as possible on shares, bonds, property and funds; woolly women spend their money on holidays, clothes and entertainment.

Switch from mindless spending to mindful spending so that you get what you want.

- Track your spending for a few weeks or months. Try to catch all of it. While it can be tedious work it usually uncovers a lot of consumption that you are unaware of.
- Make some decisions about what is really important to you and work on eliminating the mindless spending. These are your choices.
- Choose something that appeals as a proxy, like the GPG example. Find something you would prefer to have a share of than whatever it is that you are inclined to buy. If property is your thing, perhaps every latte or magazine represents a 'brick' in your investment property!

Or simply pay yourself first

If you really don't want to do the budgeting thing (the B word) and haven't got the discipline to watch your consumption closely there is another way! Women have two ways of saving: some put aside any money that is left (the surplus) when they have bought what they need or want, while others save a set amount each pay period.

The second strategy is often a much better approach simply because there is hardly anything ever left over when you do your budget. Most of us mean to save, but it doesn't always work that way. As one woman said to me, 'How come there is always so much month left at the end of the money?'

You won't even miss the money if you can decide to save the same amount each payday or whatever period works for you. Most women find it is easier to do it when they get paid, but not everybody gets her income as a wage or salary. The simplest thing to do is to set up an automatic payment to another account and have the bank make the transfer every week, month, quarter or whatever suits you. You can then use these sums for investment.

Where will this money come from? Out of your former spending, of course. You can work out the amount you can afford by nominating a sum (e.g. $100, $300) or by choosing a percentage (5%, 10%, 20%). Obviously the sums or percentages will vary depending on your income and how stretched you really are—a woman on a low income who is barely making ends meet for her basic needs is less able to pay herself a large dollar amount or a large percentage of her pay than a woman who has a high income and is a fairly extravagant consumer.

If your income is already stretched to meet your needs you should still do a very careful budget, looking to save a dollar here and a dollar there and perhaps eliminating some categories altogether. If your income is not so stressed you can simply decide on an amount that you will save each period and spend what's left! This will certainly suit women who spend until there is no more. And, assuming that you have not left the children to starve or chosen not to pay the power bill, it doesn't matter how you choose to spend the rest. The details of your spending (budget) are of no interest to anyone but you. From an investment and wealth-creation point of view, spent is spent: all that really matters is what you *don't* spend.

Paying yourself first is simple. It's a good idea to start reasonably small and build up the amounts you pay in as you become more certain that you can manage on what's left. You'll probably get more and more enthused by the idea as you see the savings start to grow. In a later chapter we'll talk about what to do with this money. For now it's enough to know that it is not spent and that it is earning you interest.

Paying yourself first is a killer strategy. If you are young enough, this strategy *alone* is probably sufficient to make you financially free over your working life because of the power of compounding and the fact that you have enough time for it to work.

It is hard to overstate the importance of compounding (and I am going to mention it several times). I find that people can easily understand the basic arithmetic but somehow overlook the power that compounding has on money—that if you leave your money in an investment and allow the interest that is earned to be reinvested your money will grow hugely over longer periods of time. Time is the best friend of the investor.

If you invested \$100 for fifty years with an annual interest rate of 10%, your investment after fifty years would only be worth \$600—your \$100 stake plus the fifty interest payments of \$10 you received each year (50 × \$10 = \$500) and spent. However, if you had reinvested the interest you earned each year your initial \$100 would have grown to almost \$12 000! When you graph the effects of compounding it is obvious:

Compounding effect

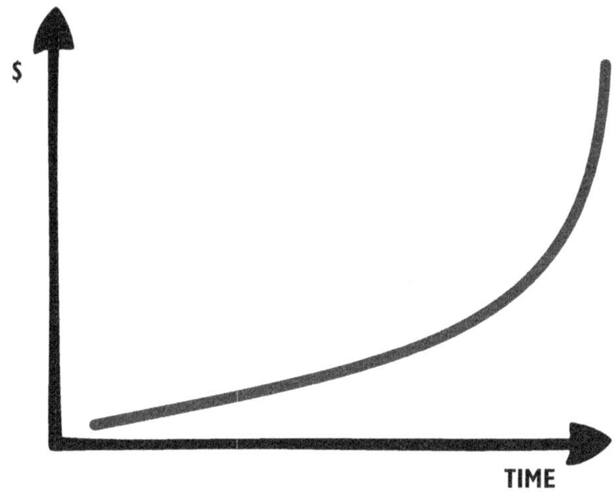

Those of us who have been earning income for twenty, thirty or more years and who failed to save from the start can only be so wise in hindsight! But if you are a young woman reading this you have just found the closest thing I know to a (legal) silver bullet for creating wealth.

Some of you who are professionals or business owners will have enough income (profits) to set aside very significant amounts of money on a regular basis. No matter what you have done so far you have the means, because of your high incomes, to catch up in the wealth-creation race. And business owners should get some money out of the business—you may be inclined to keep it all there because of the high returns you can create in your business, but it's too risky. More about investing more widely—diversification—in the chapters 'Manage your risk' (page 76) and 'How diversified should you be?' (page 158).

- Work out what you can afford to put aside on a regular basis, whether it is weekly from a wage (or the household budget), monthly from a salary, or a couple of times a year from farm payouts or dividend cheques. The important thing is to try to commit to some amount.
- Set up a separate bank account for these deposits. This money will be your investment money. Keep accumulating it until you choose an investment that suits or have enough to make a purchase.

Maximise income

If you are in paid employment (and self-employment as a contractor or consultant is only another form of job; you can't sell the business) then you should take steps to maximise that income. It is astonishing how reticent many highly skilled women are in asking for a salary increase, investigating other employment at more lucrative rates, or up-skilling themselves at their own expense in order to be more valuable in the marketplace. Even a relatively small increase in salary diverted into investments can make a great difference over a ten-year period.

Many women feel that there is little that they can do to improve their circumstances as all of their time and effort is consumed by a job or career. They look at the difficulties of becoming an investor and feel that this is way beyond their reach. Most women who have a job will need to continue to provide income from that job. The key for earning women is to create a surplus of income (either by earning more or spending less—or both!) and putting that surplus into investments.

So put some thought into increasing your income from whatever sources are available. Consider some of these:

- **Ask for a payrise.** My experience as a manager is that very few women ever do. Try it—it almost always works! And when you get it, diarise the date for asking for the next one. Inflation alone means you are going backwards in real terms unless you get regular salary increases.

- **Make yourself more valuable.** Think about what you can do to make sure your employer continues to be willing to give you increases in pay. Make yourself as useful as possible. Managers are acutely aware of how difficult it is to replace good people.
- **Market what you do.** I have observed so often that it is only when people leave that managers become aware of what they actually did. This is particularly true in the case of women who tend to do much that is behind the scenes, or for which they ask no acknowledgement. Often, when a wonderful woman leaves, insult is added to injury when she is replaced by two people! If your boss is to value you she needs to know what you actually do. So give the boss frequent updates or brief reports so that she is in no doubt about the value of your work.
- **Grow your skills.** Every business is different but you need to figure out what you need to become better at or where you could excel. This could be a 'hard' skill like spreadsheeting or a 'soft' one like dealing with complaints. Whatever you choose, do your best to be the best at something. In the end that's what employers are paying for. This is a lifelong quest and you should never stop. Yes, your workplace should be providing training and development but you own the ultimate responsibility for creating your own worth in the marketplace.
- **Look around.** Many employees never check the market. Maybe you can increase your income substan-

tially by changing jobs. Perhaps you have been underpaid for years and could make a great leap in salary. This can be particulary true if you are working in a small business where no one is keeping much of an eye on the labour market. Just letting your manager see you reading the 'Jobs Vacant' column a few times can be enough to get movement. After all, you may be very happy where you are!

If you are not in paid employment you may need to become quite inventive about getting more income. Consider these options:

- **Get a job.** You may not need to work. You may not even particularly want a paid job for its own sake. But a job may provide you quite quickly with a significant amount of money to invest.
- **Seek work at home.** Nowadays much can be done from home. Perhaps you have word processing skills. You may have the writing skills to edit the reports that many professionals write—many are excellent technically but need a lot of help to polish their work. There is a growing demand for child care, especially after school and during holidays. If you need to be home-based you can still earn significant additional income.
- **Get a boarder.** Many of you may have plenty of room to have someone to stay. Students are a good source of income and rarely infringe much on family life.
- **Get your adult children to pay board.** Many of my clients have adult children—studying or employed—

living at home. Very few of them seem to contribute much other than the odd household task. This is your choice, of course, but it represents a huge subsidy from your income to theirs. If you are not already wealthy and are struggling to release some sums for investment you should consider changing these arrangements—unless these grown-up children are committed to providing you with income in later life!

- **Sell some stuff.** Over the years we all accumulate masses of things that we no longer use or love. You might put together a tidy sum for investment by gathering all of the sports equipment, toys, books and so on that your family no longer uses and selling it on eBay or TradeMe. One of my clients has a very tidy house in spite of her three teenagers. Her rule is that anything left lying around is sold! Her teens learnt the hard way very quickly—brilliant!

Maximising your income is all about creating a surplus, no matter how large or small your income. If you are committed to creating wealth through investment then you will look hard at the income side as well as the expenditure side. For many, it is easier to find an extra dollar of income than to find an extra dollar to save.

- Consider your options about getting some additional income and take action on at least one possibility.
- Keep asking 'How can I increase my income?'

PART 3

THE PRINCIPLES OF INVESTING

It's not luck 53
There are only three investments 56
Buy investments for their yield 61
Markets are emotional 67
Manage your risk 76
You make money when you buy 90
Borrow smartly 100
Time matters 108
Superannuation 121
Getting good advice 128

It's not luck

Investment is not about rolling the dice or going to the casino or betting on the horses. Some investors do well and others do not but that is not a matter of luck. The ones who succeed do so because they follow the underlying *principles* of investment.

The following chapters outline these principles of investment. I could have called them rules or keys for investment because that is what they are. I deliberately avoided naming them tips or secrets because my experience is that too many women already think that investment is more like gambling or going to the races—someplace where you try your luck or speculate on a big win—than a principle-based activity that makes sense and works well, if you play by the rules.

Investing is all about putting your money into things that have a high chance of doing well for you in the short to medium term and an even better chance of giving you good returns in the long term. There are many things that will do that: shares, property, fixed interest and cash deposits.

You do not need to become an expert in order to be a successful investor. You do not need an advanced degree in jargon and gobbledegook in order to make sound investments. But you do need to understand and follow the basic principles.

There are no silver bullets either. Beware of anyone who promises you instant and effortless riches from your investments. Successful investment takes time and care, just like everything else worthwhile: health, relationships, children, and achievement in any field.

There is some risk involved. To invest you are going to have to give your money to someone else, even if only the bank. The alternative is to keep it under the mattress, which has its own risks. There is always a risk that you do not get your money back, but that risk is small and manageable if you stick to the rules. Many of you will be very nervous about deciding whom to trust, and rightly so. Anywhere there is money there are unscrupulous people looking to take it. However, if you stick to the principles and stay informed your risks are very low. Risk is something to be managed rather than avoided altogether, an impossible position in any area of life.

Remember that it's *your* money. You make the decisions and keep control. You can use other people to do much of the work for you but you do need to understand what is going on and you should never give up control. There is a very big difference between delegating work and management tasks, and abdicating involvement and responsibility. You should no more give away ultimate responsibility for your investments than you would for your children.

Investment is fun. The more you understand the principles the more enjoyable it is. And it is not difficult. As you read the following chapters you will realise that you already know most of this—it's just common sense. Women make great investors. They have good life experience, they are used to making pragmatic decisions, they have lots of practice being sensible. And believe it or not, the evidence is that we are far less 'emotional' than men in our investments and less likely to fall prey to tips from the brother-in-law or to take irresponsible risks in order to impress!

- What does the word 'investment' mean to you?
- What do you want to associate the word with in the future?

There are only three investments

That simplifies things immediately, doesn't it? One of the things that seems most confusing for a beginner is that everywhere you look there seems to be a bewildering array of so-called investments, from art and angora goats to zinc; and someone is urging you to put your money there.

However, the definition of an investment is that it must give you a return. This return must be in the form of income. That is, the asset must produce some return for you, like interest, rental income, or dividends. That rules out almost all of the things that are touted as investments such as art, cars, jewellery and so on. If you buy these things as an 'investment' you are simply hoping that they will appreciate in value—you are speculating that they will be worth more in the future than they are now. This is not an investment because there is no income.

Investments are also valued by their income. You have to pay more for investments that are likely to give good and growing income and that are likely to continue to do so. In this light, a commercial property in a good location with good tenants that is quality built is worth more than one that is less well built or in a poorer location or without long-term lessees, because in the first instance the rental incomes are higher and likely to continue for a long time.

Similarly, shares in a blue-chip company that makes good profits and has great brands and lots of customers are worth more than shares in a business that is struggling to make money, or hasn't got an established brand and doesn't have very many customers. When you invest, you are buying streams of income. If the income streams look like they are getting better or more sustainable then the value of the investment will also rise, so the property or shares go up in price too, and you get capital gain as well as higher income.

The only things that will give you income are:

- **Business.** You can buy all or part (shares) of a business. Your income will be in the form of profits or dividends.
- **Property.** You can buy all or part of rental property. Your income will be in the form of rents.
- **Interest-bearing deposits/cash.** You lend your money to a bank or business (bonds) or other entity (government bonds, securities) and they pay you for using your money. Your income is in the form of interest.

All true investments are either one of these or a means of investing in one of these. You'll see advertisements for managed funds, unit trusts, hedge funds and so on. These are *ways* of investing in business, property or deposits. For example, you might buy units (shares) in a trust that invests in commercial property because you can't afford to buy the whole property, or because you want to own a tiny bit of several commercial properties (to spread your risk), or because you want to invest in property but you don't want anything to do with the management of it because you may lack the time or the skills.

The focus of investment is to get a return from the assets you buy. Calculating your return is simple arithmetic (see below).

- Scan the media to see what kinds of investments are being advertised. Get comfortable with working out what the underlying investment is—business, property or deposits.
- Note what kind of income is advertised—regular dividends, interest payments, etc.
- Note what levels of returns are suggested.

Equity and debt

Some investments buy you a piece of the company whereas others get you a promise of repayment. If you buy some investments you get equity, or ownership, of some or all of the investment. This is what happens when you buy shares. What you get back depends on how well the company does and how many shares you own.

If you lend money, as you do when you buy a bond, you have made an investment in *debt*. You have lent your money in return for the payment of interest to you and the promise that you will get your money back. You will know when you can expect to get your money back (the maturity date) and you will be fairly sure of how much interest you will earn (unless the borrower defaults). Knowing how much your money will earn and when you'll receive it makes debt investments attractive for many borrowers.

If you buy funds (or, more accurately, shares in a fund), you may be buying equity or debt investments, or a combination of both. If the fund earns interest or dividends on these investments, it will pay your share as a distribution. It is important to know what your fund invests in—the fund itself is just a kind of 'packaging' for a range of investments.

Rate of return (ROR)

Returns—what you get out of your investment—matter. The real rate of return is what you get after tax and inflation. It's a good idea to get used to working this out. Sometimes it's hard to get a real rate of return, for example, if inflation is running away (as some of you will remember in the 1980s) or if taxation rates are high (they have been higher in the past). Many people in the 1980s were losing money on their investments: I know lots of older people who had most of their money in the bank. Inflation was eroding the value of their deposits faster than the interest rate, so every month they left their money there they got poorer!

Calculating the real rate of return is simple arithmetic. You subtract the rate of tax and the rate of inflation from your return. You need to use percentages for all the numbers. Your return is called 'yield' when it is written as a percentage.

Yield	9%
Less tax (33%)	(3%)
Return after tax	6%
Less inflation	(2%)
Real rate of return	**4%**

This investor is getting a 9% yield (return) on her investments in property, shares and deposits. However, after she has paid tax (at 33%) and accounted for inflation (2%) she has a **real rate of return of only 4%**. This means that she is getting 4% wealthier each year.

Buy investments for their yield

Capital gain matters, but the income or yield from your investments matters even more. Income is usually called 'yield' when it is expressed as a percentage. If you buy just because you think that the asset will be worth more in the future then you are speculating rather than investing. It is the ability to generate income that distinguishes investments from speculation or gambling.

Income matters for several reasons. First of all it gives you a return on your investment. The jargon used changes from type to type—profits and dividends from shares, interest from deposits and rentals from property. As the yield goes up the value of the asset usually rises (and conversely, the value falls if the income falls). This is where you get your capital gain. So if you buy an investment that gives good yield you will usually get capital growth as well. Investments are valued for their yield and you should watch it carefully and value it, too.

So when you are considering investments you need to know what income they have, and you need to know what kind of yield you should expect from that particular type of asset. This is much easier to do with some investments than others. For example, it's quite simple to find out what the income for a property is. You simply ask the owner or real estate agent what the rent is. It can be harder with shares. You can easily find out what last year's profits were, but what about next year or the year after? And the rent from the property could be misleading. Maybe they are paying above the market and a rent review is due, at which time the rental will drop.

The past is also a poor guide to the future. We all have brilliant investment strategies in hindsight but the only income that matters is the income that is still to come. So historical profits or dividends or rentals can be a guide or give you some insight, but you'll have to work a bit harder to make a sound estimate of what the future will bring. This is where you will have to make some effort to keep up with what's happening in the economy—are we heading for better times or a recession? What's happening to interest rates and what will that do to your prospective investments? You will need to read the business pages and perhaps some material from your broker or professionals or from investment associations that you join. This information will not give you tips: by the time it's in print everyone will know it and it's too late to move, but you need to know it too. You'll still get surprises good and bad: some companies will announce lucrative new contracts that drive their profits and share value up, whereas others will lose a CEO or have a product recall and the opposite will happen.

Figuring out what yield you should get is another matter. As a beginner you may well wonder why one investment should expect a 5% yield while another may fairly expect a 15% yield. The market decides what is a fair value for each investment. There are enough buyers and sellers in most markets for us to 'agree' on what should be paid. This is not an exact science, but it basically comes down to how well investors (the market) regard the future prospects of this investment, and how safe they think the investment is.

Have you ever wondered why finance companies pay much higher rates of interest on deposits than a bank? It's because your money is less secure. So if Australasian Bank Incorporated, that has billions of dollars in backing and has been around for 200 years and is triple AAA rated, is offering 7% on your deposit, you are going to want more return (yield) than that to invest your money with Bloggs Financial Enterprises that was set up three years ago. You might require 10% or even 12% to compensate for the additional risk you are taking.

The principle is the same with property. A relatively low quality rental property in Villageville (8-10%) will usually yield more than a premium property on the High Street (5-7%) because you are not going to get any capital gain in Villageville and the location is less desirable for tenants and other investors. Investors will accept a lower yield from an investment that they think is likely to grow or looks more sustainable (or secure) over time.

I took a distressing phone call from an older woman when the first of the finance company collapses finally made the news. She was distraught, and she had good reason to be. She was living on a small superannuation income and was making ends meet by being very frugal, as many older women have to.

financial companies because of the advertised interest rates which were a couple of points above her bank's. The difference in income was significant for her. However, knowing almost nothing about investment, she did not understand the much greater risk she was taking with her money. At the time of writing I cannot be sure what, if anything, she will get back of her savings but she will certainly lose a substantial amount. This is a huge blow. Needless to say, she has no means of replacing this capital and her future income will be even smaller than it was before.

For your investments to rise in value you need to find ones that will grow their income, or ones that look so good to other investors that they will be happy to accept a lower yield in the future. In other words, the investment will be rated 'up' to a lower yield.

During the property boom that has been going on worldwide for the last few years, the value of properties has soared. Interestingly, rentals have risen very little. Investors, instead, have been prepared to accept much lower yields with many properties selling on 4-5% yields when they previously attracted 7-9%. Time will tell whether the investors are right.

Calculating yield

Yield compares the earnings (income, rent) to the purchase price of the investment. Yield and the value of the investment are the two sides of the same idea. Investors will want a higher yield from a poorer quality investment because the expectations of future capital gain or future profits are lower. You can only get a higher yield by:

a) getting a higher income (more interest, higher rental, bigger dividend); or
b) the price of the investment falling.

$$\text{Yield} = \frac{\text{Income} \times 100}{\text{Value of investment}}$$

Likewise, the value is determined by the income. So for the value to rise, either:

a) the income must rise; or
b) the market must accept a lower yield.

$$\text{Value of investment} = \frac{\text{Income} \times 100}{\text{Appropriate yield}}$$

So, typically, a poorer quality property will provide rentals (yield) at a higher percentage of the property's value than a better quality property. For the property to increase in value either the rents (income) have to rise or the buyers have to be happy to pay more for the same stream of rentals, i.e. they have to be prepared to accept a lower yield.

It's a good idea to play around with these calculations on some properties or shares you are looking at so that you become familiar with the idea. The arithmetic is simple but the ideas may be new to you.

Markets are emotional

You could make markets sound hysterical, always jittery, always moving, always reacting to the latest tidbit of information. This doesn't mean that they are right or wrong. It just means that there are lots of players and someone is always ready to buy and someone is always ready to sell. The numbers on either side of the table change by the minute as individual investors change their views on a particular investment and the prices go up and down, sometimes by the minute. You can watch this happening over the Internet. It's great fun, especially when you are thinking about buying or selling particular shares. Property is doing the same, of course. You just can't see it because no one is making an offer every day to buy and sell, but if they did we would see the prices move up and down all the time.

Markets seem emotional because the individual players are: sometimes the markets are very high and we have a boom because there is a feeling of optimism or even hype around and it infects most of the players. If the opposite happens we have gloom and possibly recession. The market moves freely and quickly. It is not always 'right'; things may be overpriced but it corrects sooner or later.

It is all this uncertainty that makes it both nerve-racking and exciting. You are free to buy or sell, but there is always someone who thinks the opposite. Otherwise there would be no seller or buyer to work with to create a market.

The markets keep shifting from day to day. It can generate a frenzy—you'll have seen pictures of brokers yelling their trades on the old live trading floors. It's all done electronically now but the excitement and panic will be the same. Emotion is infectious and, just like individuals, the market overreacts both up and down. You need to know this so you can keep your head. As you will know with other areas of life, it is difficult to maintain a course when public opinion is against you. These overreactions lead to both bull (driving upwards) and bear (clawing downwards) cycles.

The market moves up and down frequently, even daily. The important thing to remember is that you should take a longer-term view, and markets grow over time.

The market

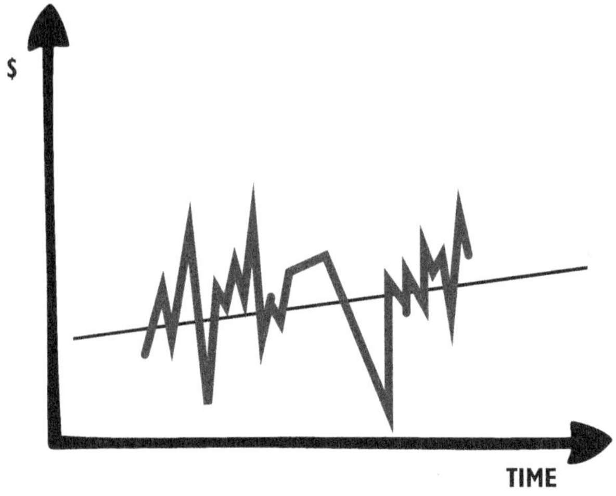

It's easy to get unnerved as you watch your investments. However, in many ways this uncertainty is great: if you can keep your head and think through your principles of investment, then there is great money to be made in both bull and bear cycles. There is an old Wall Street adage that bulls make money, bears make money, but pigs never do. In other words, it's a warning about getting carried away by greed.

Markets operate on information. As soon as anything is known or expected, the prices move accordingly—the information is factored in almost instantly. The sharemarket is usually ahead of events because investors are already pricing in their expectations and anticipations. But the markets often overreact and the expectations are sometimes wrong. Again, you'll have to do your own thinking and learn to manage your own emotional turmoil.

In theory, markets are efficient. The price of everything reflects all of the information available; that is, all of the facts and expectations are already 'priced in'. It's right up to a point but there are always 'bargains' just like in every other field. These will be investments that, for whatever reason, are not fully priced because they are not fashionable or the business media have been ignoring them, or the 'story' doesn't sell well. It's your job to find these bargains that are waiting to be discovered.

It's a little paradoxical but you need to both watch the markets (and the underlying aspects of the economy, particularly industries you are interested in investing in and specific companies or properties that you might buy) and at the same time you need to stand apart, and remain a little aloof. You have to keep sniffing the air and gauging the mood as this will affect your investments, but you must avoid getting infected with whatever fever is doing the rounds. Intelligent investment is about using your head rather than being swayed by your heart. That does not mean that there are not wonderful investments in 'good' things that do well for humanity and the planet; it just means that you still need to apply all the other principles of investments as well.

It's easy to make a decision for the longer term, like buying property or shares and then finding that your investment dropped in value. The $300 000 property is now worth $260 000, or the share fund that you put $10 000 into is now worth $8000. You may become despondent or panicked. It's hard to hold your nerve, but if you made a sensible choice in the first place you are probably still correct. One thing is sure, if you exit now you are sure of a loss. You are, after all, trying to buy at a low price and sell at a high one—not the other way around. You may of course have made a bad decision, at which point it's as well to recognise your poor thinking and cut your losses. Or you may simply need to rebalance your portfolio—your asset allocation may no longer be right.

Generally, you should not be buying and selling frequently unless you are choosing to be a trader rather than an investor. That's a different game altogether. You need a great deal more skill for this and need to devote yourself to the job. Buying and selling frequently is also expensive. You will have to pay fees each time. This mounts up and will affect your returns. It is very expensive to buy and sell property, and so you need to be sure about your investments.

Market highs and lows

You must be careful not to jump in and out of the markets on a whim, usually at just the wrong time!

The market (and the economy) tends to work in big cycles—money gets tighter, interest rates rise, share prices fall, property values fall, money gets easier . . . and the cycle reverses out. It never works exactly like that and it can be very difficult to anticipate the timing of the shifts; however, in general terms, it does happen like this and the cycles repeat over and over. Boom and gloom follow each other over and over.

Market cycle

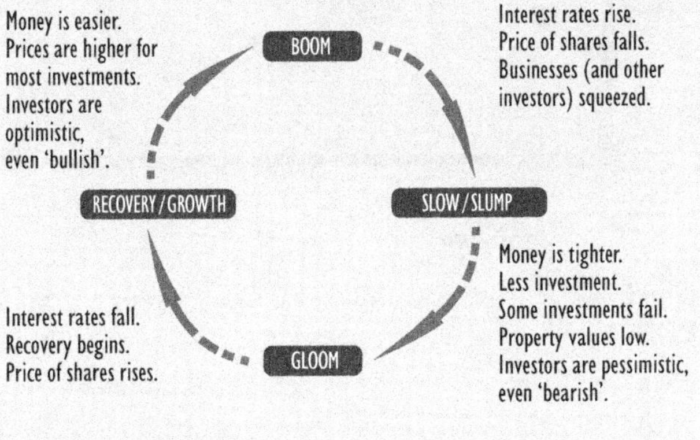

Inexperienced investors can easily be spooked by these cycles, and do exactly the wrong thing. It's very easy to get carried away by hype in boom times and put money into the market when it is at its peak. It's also very common for investors to flee from the market when it's at the bottom of the cycle, in fact at the time when good investments are going at very cheap prices!

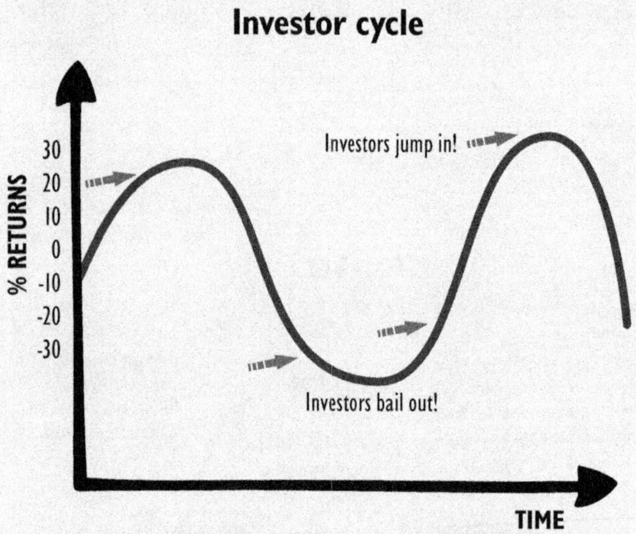

Hold on to the bigger picture. It will keep your feet on the ground. Start to see these cycles—changing times—for what they are. If you can keep your head when others are losing theirs you can avoid paying too much for investments (in boom times) and you can acquire some great assets at very low prices in the gloomy days of the market. This is where it really helps to have a plan so that you can behave in an objective way and help yourself to avoid following the herd (much more about how to plan your investments later).

Buy low and sell high

Smart investors try to behave differently than most others in the market. They discipline themselves to do the exact opposite of the typical investor cycle.

When the markets are booming, and everyone else is climbing on board in case they miss out, smart investors take their profits and sell. Yes, the market may not have peaked but they operate on the principle that they have made good returns and they try to avoid being greedy. It's always a good idea to leave something for the next person!

When markets are depressed and most other investors are bailing out is a very good time to buy investments. It often takes courage to spend when all are in gloom and predicting even darker days. However, this is when you can buy great assets at sale prices. Think of it like going shopping on Boxing Day—everything is marked down, including the very best brands, because people have spent their money buying things at inflated prices coming up to

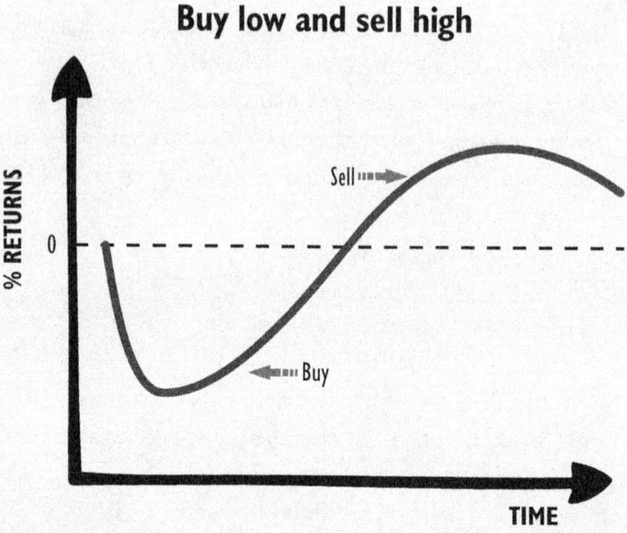

Christmas. It really pays to keep some money for opportunities like this.

Again, lots of planning and forethought really helps you behave smartly. When you do your homework about what the 'right' price is to pay for a certain share or property (or anything else for that matter), you can act quickly when it becomes available. You don't have to dither and wonder what other investors are thinking because you have done your preparation and you can grab that bargain.

Similarly, your preparation and planning will tell you that returns are high for other assets—too high, perhaps—

and it's time to sell out even though everyone else seems in a buying frenzy. In practice this will mean that you are not trying to buy at the very bottom or sell at the very top as there is no way of determining those moments except in hindsight. Instead, what it means is that you will buy when you see prices moving up after they appear to have hit the bottom and you will sell when prices are still rising but probably have not peaked. So you won't get the last dollar out of each investment. Trying to do that usually involves too much risk. It's better to be satisfied with buying some bargains and selling good profits, rather than holding out for the last cent. That can be a very expensive strategy. Remember that both bulls and bears make money but pigs get slaughtered!

Manage your risk

Risk is one of the least understood aspects of investment. This is partly because we use the word every day in a very loose way. Risk is not a single thing when you are speaking about investment; rather, risk means several specific, and differing, things in investment. Don't stop reading! You are far more likely to be comfortable with the risks you are facing and have strategies for managing them if you keep reading, and it's actually quite straightforward when you think about it.

Some of the risks that you need to consider are described below.

Default risk

The first return you should care about is the return of your money. Default risk is the risk that you might not get your capital back, never mind any income. As I write, several finance companies have collapsed; many investors will not get their money back and for some of them this will be devastating. The extra few percentage points of interest that these companies were offering don't look so great now.

This example underlines the rule that higher returns are accompanied by higher risk. However, it is clearly a mistake to take little or no risk. When choosing investments you need to do your homework. If you are investing in shares, for example, you would manage your default risk by checking that the company did not have borrowings that were too high (debt to equity ratio) and that it had enough earnings before interest and tax (EBIT) to cover its interest payments on its debt. You would also check its cash flow, i.e. is there plenty of cash flowing in to cover the costs of doing business? If the market isn't happy with the company, other investors will already have re-rated the share price down. You will need to take particular care, however, when buying shares in a smaller business or one that is not traded a lot to make sure that your money is not at risk.

> I was out walking with a group the other day. When Linda, a woman I had never met before, heard what I do professionally she asked my opinion on some property she was hoping to sell. We chatted for a while and then she said that she was hoping to 'lend' the money to her son. He is an engineer and is developing some super-duper engine. I tried, probably unsuccessfully, to hide my horror! This money represented Linda's entire investment stake and she had told me she is not a high earner. The risk of default is obvious: even with the best will in the world this enterprise is highly likely to fail. Not only is Linda unlikely to ever see a return but she is also very likely to lose her capital as well. Even if the enterprise does well, she is not getting any shares for her loan so she is totally exposed to the downside. I felt uneasy about introducing such dark thoughts but I wanted to save Linda a walk straight into default.

Liquidity risk

This is the risk that you might not be able to sell your investment when you want to for 'fair market value'. It's easy to sell most shares or to get out of many funds, but you could find yourself stuck with a particular property. It can also be difficult to sell shares that are 'thinly traded', that is, that have few buyers and sellers. So you have a risk that you can't sell or can only sell at a poor price. Small businesses can give very high returns but are often illiquid investments. You can best manage this risk by staying out of such areas or by allocating only a small part of your investment portfolio to things with low liquidity.

Many clients who have family businesses get trapped in low liquidity investments. Many of these enterprises are set up as partnerships, between brothers or friends or a wider family group. However, unless there are buy-sell agreements—agreements forcing some to buy and others to sell—these shares can be next to worthless. No one outside the family is going to buy them. Why would anyone get involved? In addition, you may not be able to collect any dividends or profits. The business can be managed to produce little or no profits and, unless there is a specified agreement for payouts, all profits can be reinvested by whoever holds the management responsibility.

Market risk

Your investments might perform poorly for all kinds of reasons beyond your control. Just about anything you can think of happening in the world can affect your investment: political decisions, wars, pandemics, terrorism, drought, oil prices, currencies, global warming and so on. You can't influence these events but you can lessen the risk to you by diversifying your portfolio to take account of your exposure to these risks (more later).

Maureen is a farmer. She knew she needed to get some investments other than the farm. Her husband was not too interested in anything beyond agriculture—and his farm in particular—but he agreed to come to a meeting. Maureen had put quite a lot of work into planning her investments and just wanted to check out her thinking before proceeding. Partly to allay her husband's criticism and partly because it was what was familiar, Maureen was proposing to buy some local rental properties as they lived close to a major farming town and there was quite a market for tenants. She also knew the agricultural sector thoroughly and had identified farm supply companies and veterinary pharmaceutical businesses that she thought were sound. I felt very bad about having to advise her to do just the opposite, but her investment strategy had a lot of market risk.

New Zealand and Australia have a very strong primary sector—much of the economy relies on income from the farming sector. Farmers are exposed to every risk under the sun, literally as well as figuratively. Everything from drought to disease to commodity prices and fluctuating currencies affects their returns. Many farmers have learnt the hard way that they need to diversify away from farming. However, they often show an alarming tendency to buy investment in related industries—farm suppliers, veterinary pharmaceuticals, property in the same region as their farm. This is understandable in some ways. They are investing in things they understand and find interesting, however the same market risks that will 'take out' the farm will also adversely affect related businesses. Imagine what happens to farm suppliers and property prices in an area that suffers a severe drought or gets foot-and-mouth disease!

So, even though it was back to the drawing board and Maureen would need to explore new areas of investment, I advised her to look at property well beyond their region and to look at shares in other industries entirely. Because they were already so exposed to the fortunes of their own country—everything tied up in land and in agriculture—I advised her to put most of the investment offshore as they needed this diversification as a hedge against anything bad happening onshore.

Specific risk

Every investment you make will carry risk specific to that investment: the bank might collapse (Barings did) or a product may be recalled because it is defective or harmful, taking the share price (and sometimes even the business) down with it. You may buy property in an area where values collapse—a factory may close or a natural disaster may wreck the local economy for years. Again, you can lessen the risk to your investment portfolio by diversification.

People work hard to build their knowledge about their investment. However, expertise and familiarity can blind you to the obvious. If anyone suggested that you should take everything you own and invest it in one share on the stockmarket you would think they were crazy. Yet that is exactly what the owners of many small businesses do: all of their money is in the business and they work there, too. You might argue that you know the business well, that it's as sound as a bell and that you are taking very good care of your eggs in this one basket. However, a key customer can leave, you can lose a major contract, a trusted employee may defraud you or a key employee may get sick. Any number of things can wreck even the most solid looking business. Look at the employees of Enron: it was touted as a world-beating business. The employees not only lost their jobs but many of them had all of their superannuation in Enron shares—worthless! You need a range of shares or a range of properties, and preferably a range of both, to safeguard against specific risk. If you have everything in your own business or farm you need to get some investment diversification. The same rule applies if you have a career or profession and have shares in the firm, or have all of your superannuation funds invested in your employer.

Volatility risk

Volatility means up and down—and even all over the place! Volatility risk means that your investment returns could vary hugely from period to period—5%, 10%, 15%, 50%, up or down on the period before. When investors say that high return means high risk it is this kind of risk they are talking about. You do not need to worry much about this if you are investing for the long term, e.g. buying investments to fund your retirement in twenty or thirty years. With that amount of time in hand you will go through several market cycles and have ample opportunity to sell at a good time. Volatility, however, can really affect your returns if you are investing for less than ten years. The best way to manage this risk is to have a diversified portfolio.

Managing volatility risk

The more volatile the investment the more it can be up or down from a steady rate of return. The problem is that if you choose to avoid all volatile investments you will miss out on some of the best investments. This is not a sensible

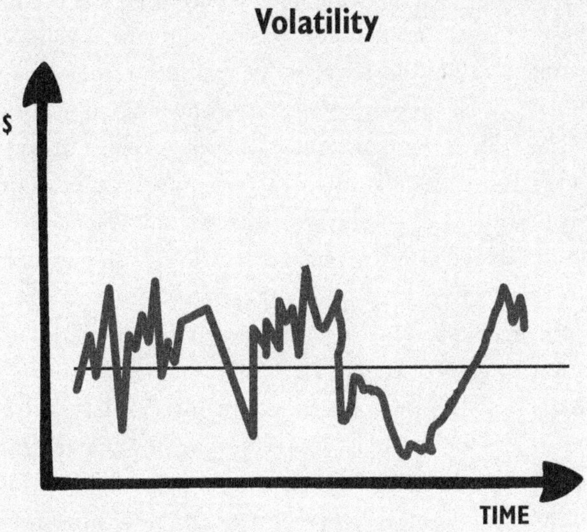

way to deal with this risk. After all, risking nothing is a risk in itself! And it is very important to keep in mind that investments that give higher growth rates (like shares and property) are more volatile, but that it would be a huge mistake to exclude them entirely from your investment portfolio in the belief that they are too 'risky'. In fact, the younger you are the more 'risky' it would be to leave them out because your real risk is that your investments will not grow enough over the years to buy you whatever you want for the future.

On the other hand, chasing the higher returns tends to bring volatility risk that could potentially wipe you out or lose a lot of your money. This is especially true if you are investing over the shorter term, i.e. you need this money within the next ten years. Volatility matters much less—is less of a risk to your investment—over a longer period.

The answer, once again, is to diversify. This time your diversification is attempting to smooth out volatility by choosing a mix of investments that will give the greatest return for a given level of risk. Economists only worked this out mathematically in recent decades. It is still called Modern Portfolio Theory.

The basic idea is to choose investments that have a low correlation—for example, it is common for the returns from bonds to be low when sharemarkets are high and for the return from bonds to be good when the returns from shares are low. This does not always work precisely but the principle is correct. If you can choose a portfolio with investments that have a low correlation then the *average* volatility of your portfolio is lowered.

For any given acceptable level of risk there will be an optimal portfolio (mix) of investments that will give the best returns for that particular level of risk. Fund managers use advanced software to work out the mix. This is beyond the scope of the private investor but it is the principle that you should try to follow. The set of portfolios that give the best returns at each level of risk form a curve when graphed. This is called the efficient frontier and looks like this:

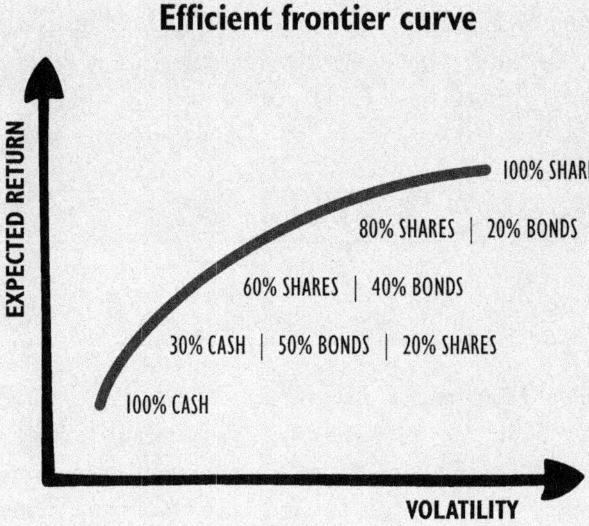

So, for example, cash gives lower returns but the returns don't jump around. You can be fairly certain of what you will get if you put your money in your bank account—but it won't be much, a few percentage points. Shares can give you much higher returns—15% or more—but it could be much more or much *much* less! Getting the right mix for your circumstances is important. The question is, how much return do you need and how much volatility risk can you afford to take?

And never forget your time frames—the real risk of volatility is in the short term. People tend to underestimate this and do mad things like putting their tax money in the sharemarket for the next six months. It could disappear! On the other hand, people overestimate volatility risk in the longer term—it would be equally daft to avoid growth assets like property and shares if your time horizon is a decade or more.

Diversification

I have recommended diversification as the way to manage most of the risks above. So what does it mean? Literally, it is about spreading your investments around so that you do not put all of your eggs in one basket. Once you consider the concept it is clearly common sense, otherwise you are staking everything on a single play, whether that's your own business, farm, an equity stake in someone else's business, a very small range of shares or a property portfolio that's concentrated in one place.You can take the idea even further and think about how small New Zealand and/or Australia are in the global scheme of things and how easily single adverse events would send our economies down.

The principle behind the advice to diversify is to spread your risks widely so that it will take near-global level catastrophe to wipe out your investments.

Each person's needs will be different because each of you will have a different mix of risks depending on your personal circumstances and what assets you already hold. You can be too widely diversified—if your assets are spread too thinly they may achieve very average returns as a result. In addition, you will have far too much work to do to administer or supervise your portfolio.

The best way to approach this is to consider the liabilities/risks you personally face. Ask the 'what if' questions.

What would happen to my investments if:

- NZ/Aus/both got foot-and-mouth disease?
- a natural disaster affected the region I live in?
- the NZ/Aus currencies took a dive?
- the bank I use collapsed?
- tourism ceased owing to terror/pandemic/ oil prices?
- I have a significant default risk?
- I have a significant liquidity risk?
- a particular market gets in trouble?
- a particular bank, institution or business collapses?

I am not trying to frighten you, but to encourage you to look at where your wealth is, and to make sure that it is not exposed to a king-hit like one of the above. It is very common for people to own a home, have a business, farm or job in the same area and also have their investments in allied areas—local property or shares in connected businesses. It made sense when you were doing it: this is where I am and intend to be; this is what I know and like; I can manage all this because it is familiar and close and I have inside expertise. Everything about that makes sense, particularly as you build it up over time, but the whole edifice is very vulnerable to single disruptive events.

So to state what now must be obvious:

- You need to have some of your investments offshore (see the chapter 'How much should you have offshore?' on page 162).
- You need investments outside the region you live and/or work in.
- You need some countercyclical investments, things that are likely to be up when other assets you have are down.

Risk is one of those catch-all words that we use without thinking: take the idea a little further and ask what some of your personal 'liabilities' might be, the particular risks that you have some exposure to. I travel to Ireland to work and to catch up with my (very large!) Irish family several times each year. I am therefore 'exposed' to a drop in the value of the New Zealand dollar relative to the euro in particular. It makes sense to hedge that liability, to hold euros or to hold shares denominated in euros. It won't prevent the dollar from dropping but it will at least allow me to buy a coffee (or a Guinness) when next in Dublin. Many of you will have similar liabilities: family overseas, future plans for travel, particular health issues or other concerns.

A word of caution: diversification is about managing down your risk by spreading your bets. Some of you, however, should ignore this advice! Diversification cuts your returns as well as your risk. If you are relatively young, you can (and probably should) take the risks—you have decades to get it right and recover from negative events. Similarly, those who have specialised knowledge are often in a position to take a strong stand in some particular investment, for example, you may know a great deal about retail, gold, agriculture or property. Just don't bet *everything* on it as you need enough to start again if necessary!

You make money when you buy

As in so many other areas of life, you need to get it right at the start of any investment. In a nutshell, you have to buy quality. This is more obvious with some investments than with others, but the principle applies to all of them. Quality assets perform better in good times; in less than favourable times they hold their value better. Superior assets win both ways: they give you better returns and they are safer. This is not about the price you pay, because you will have to pay well for assets that are considered good. Sometimes you will get a 'bargain', a quality asset that the market has not recognised as quickly as you or which is not selling for some reason.

So, how do you figure out what you should buy? A quality asset is an asset that will give you good and sustainable income that will grow. That is how you should evaluate investments. This is easily forgotten in boom periods. There was a frenzy, for example, at the end of the last century about technology stocks and around businesses that were Internet based. College students were 'floating' businesses on the basis of a couple of pages of a 'plan'. Many normally rational investors bought into the idea that 'the Internet changes everything', as Bill Gates said. Well, the Internet has changed a lot of things, and I for one would hate to be without it. But it did not change the fundamental principles of investment and the fact that your investments must give you a return. Most of these so-called Internet stocks never made a dollar profit, much less distributed dividends to shareholders. Making any money through them relied on the 'greater fool theory'. You buy at a given price in the hope that an even greater idiot will pay you even more to take it away from you soon after! Booms are made of thinking (or lack of same!) and market emotion like this. You might get lucky if you are very fast and your timing is just right, but this kind of behaviour is not investing. It is speculating and gambling.

These kinds of booms are often caused by too much money. Markets are very high as I write at the end of 2006 for much the same reason: there is a lot of investment cash looking for a home. When people can't find a quality investment they often buy a poor one. It's often not obvious until there is a bit of a downturn. Then the share prices drop, the buildings are untenanted and the poor investments are exposed. Low quality assets are much more volatile. They can rocket or plummet in price, so there is money to be made if you can take the risk attached to that. However, this is best left to traders and speculators. As a smart woman investor you should stick to buying quality assets to get the best performance over time and to manage your risks well.

Over the longer term you will do better with quality property and shares. See 'The arithmetic of quality' (page 93) to work out the way the arithmetic is done. Again, while the jargon may be new, the sums are really simple. The concepts and underlying principles make perfect sense once you apply this to anything you own or have invested in before now.

You should also apply the same quality principle to interest-bearing deposits or anything you put your money into in order to collect interest. Banks pay the lowest rates of interest. That's because they carry the least risk in this part of the world. That of course is not necessarily the case with banks everywhere. You have to make a judgement about the quality of the institution that you are lending your money to and how secure that money is, i.e. how likely you are to get your money back. As the interest rates climb for other deposits—bonds, finance companies—the risks are higher. Most institutions carry some kind of rating from an external agency. The lower the rating the higher the interest they will have to pay to get investors to lend them money. This does not always work perfectly: the Bank of New Zealand almost failed in 1989. And many people who had HIH bonds lost their money. Bonds are usually considered a lower risk than shares because bondholders are paid out before shareholders. Beware second and third tier finance companies. It is very difficult to judge their creditworthiness. They pay high interest for a reason and you need to understand your risk. For example, as I write Provincial Finance Ltd have just gone into receivership in New Zealand.

Security is the second issue—remember default risk. When you borrow money, the bank will take a security over your home (a mortgage) so that if you do not repay the loan they will take the house. When you lend, the boot is on the other foot. Very creditworthy borrowers, like the government, leading banks or big businesses, won't give you any security over their assets, but smaller businesses and finance companies usually do. This is called a debenture, which means that you get paid out before creditors or lenders who have no security. You are higher up in the queue of people who are looking to get their money back if the borrower fails. And there are different levels of debenture. The second and third tier debenture holders have to wait in line behind the first tier. So, I would recommend that even if you are tempted by some of these interest rates, you read the detail carefully. If you still feel that you want to invest, make sure that it is a very small proportion of your money that you lend. Many unsophisticated investors get burned in this way. It is very sad to see an older person who needed this interest return to live on lose all her money just because she did not understand that flashy advertising fronted by faces she recognised from TV did not mean a thing in terms of credit worthiness of the company or the security of her money.

While you do not want to become paralysed by nerves and indecision, most of your efforts need to go into the purchasing decision. If you get that right you have little to do except wait for your returns and work on choosing what investments to buy next!

The arithmetic of quality

Investments are valued by income. This is done by applying a 'multiplier' to the income (e.g. multiplying income by a number such as 5, 10 or 15). This multiplier is called different things for different investment classes, for example, for shares it's a P:E ratio and for property a yield.

It's very easy to illustrate this with shares. The P:E (price to earnings) ratio is the number of times the price is greater than the earnings each year. So if a share has a P:E of ten it means that you have to pay ten times the earnings of a share (earnings per share—eps) to buy a share, so if each share earned 10c last year the price of the share is $1. The value of the earnings of a share varies from one company to another. Sounds strange—10c here is not as valuable as 10c there? That's right. A quality company will have a higher P:E; for example, Blue Chip company may have a P:E of fifteen, in which case you will have to pay $1.50 for a share that earns 10c. The Ordinary Average company share that produces eps of 10c will have a P:E of about ten—you'll have to pay $1 for those earnings. A lower quality Dog Tucker company, whose prospects are not considered too rosy, might have a P:E of five—you can get earnings or a dividend of 10c for the purchase of a share for 50c. This can seem upside down at first, but is common sense when you think about it. The better company is likely to have a more sustainable stream of profits or dividends, and the future is brighter, so we expect more upside. The poorer company is a greater risk (or rather its earnings for the future are less certain), and so the shares are less valuable. The marketplace, i.e. buyers and sellers, make this decision each day as they decide what price they will buy or sell at.

You win both ways as an investor in quality shares. Every dollar extra that the Blue Chip company makes in profits is valued by that multiple of fifteen and the share price will continue to rise. Even if two companies have the same dollar amount of increase in earnings, the one with the higher P:E ratio will see a bigger rise in its share price because the market will value this extra profit more highly and bid the share price up.

Let's say all companies start with the same share price:

	share price	**P:E ratio**	**earnings per share (eps)**
Dog Tucker	200c	5	40c
Ordinary Average	200c	10	20c
Blue Chip	200c	15	13c

Each of these companies has different earnings per share. You may or may not be receiving these as dividends—they may be retained by the company. Now look what happens to the share price if the earnings per share of each company rose by 5c.

	old share price	**P:E ratio**	**old eps**	**new eps**	**new share price**	**% change**
Dog Tucker	200c	5	40c	45c	225c	+12½%
Ordinary Average	200c	10	20c	25c	250c	+25%
Blue Chip	200c	15	13c	18c	270c	+35%

The better quality company saw its share price rise by 35% compared to 25% for the average company and 10% for the low quality company. Of course, it's never as straightforward as this. The better company is also likely to have faster earnings growth as well, but it is easier to grasp the principle if you only change one thing at a time. Note too that the actual price of a share is largely irrelevant and you can't tell very much from it because you don't know what the earnings are or how many shares the company has issued. A share might be a bargain at $20 or be a bad buy at $2 or even a snip at $200! What really matters is the P:E, how the market multiplies the earnings to set the price.

Property is valued in the same way but the jargon is, of course, different. Property is valued by its yield (also called the capitalisation or cap rate). The multiplier used on the income is the reciprocal (or inverse; divide into 100) of the yield. So if a property has a yield of 8% you multiply the annual rent by 12.5 to establish the value of the property. If the property had a yield of 12.5% the property is only worth eight times its rental income. Remember that quality properties have lower yield because the rents are more sustainable and you usually get good capital growth as well.

So:

	rent	yield	reciprocal of yield	value
Great location	$10 000	8%	12.5	$125 000
Ordinary property	$10 000	10%	10	$100 000
Dump	$10 000	12.5%	8	$80 000

If you could get the rent up on each of these properties, look what happens to the value of the property:

	rent	yield	reciprocal of yield	value
Great location	$12 500	8%	12.5	$156 250
Ordinary property	$12 500	10%	10	$125 000
Dump	$12 500	12.5%	8	$100 000

A rise in rent of $2500 has given the better quality property a capital gain of $31 250, while the average property only grew by $25 000 and the low quality one by $20 000. Again, it's never as simple as this in practice. In fact, the quality property is likely to see rents rise faster than the poorer property so these effects tend to be even greater.

Because of bad experiences with the sharemarket in 1987 and again in 2000 many women perceive shares as especially risky. This is not so and you would be unwise to abandon shares altogether. But it does highlight that discussions around risk can be very emotive rather than rational. You do really have to engage your rational side in these discussions.

Much of the risk in investment is about volatility, how much the value of your investments go up and down (fluctuate or oscillate) over time. Investments giving higher returns are usually more volatile. You can compensate for this by having investments that are countercyclical, or ones that go up when others go down.

Reversion to mean

Yet another aspect of the idea of quality or the appropriate P:E ratio for a share or yield for a property is the idea that markets revert to the mean. A mean is just another word for an average. This concept suggests that there is an appropriate 'band' within which certain qualities of properties or businesses should sit. Sometimes their market prices will seem very high and at other times they will be priced well below those historical averages. The concept of reversion to mean suggests that sooner or later they will return to their appropriate band. For example, shares in quality companies have historically traded at an average P:E ratio of 12–15. If a particular share, or the market in general, is trading on much higher averages you should expect a reversion—a correction—to the longer term average some time soon. There will always be someone to tell you why these times are like no others before. But they said that during Tulipmania in the 1920s, in the 1980s, and as recently as the end of the twentieth century about technology stocks. History says they are wrong—markets always revert to the mean, it's just really hard to pick the day and the hour. Buyer beware!

Borrow smartly

We have mixed feelings and all kinds of meanings attached to the idea of borrowing. Many of you will have been brought up with 'never a borrower nor a lender be'. The very word 'owe' tends to have negative connotations; 'debt' is laden with meaning. You are likely to know that running up credit card debt and borrowing money for consumption—holidays, entertainment, clothes—is very bad practice and ruinous to your finances. But what about other borrowing? Most of us would never own a home without borrowing to buy one as we could never accumulate the necessary amount to pay cash. And should you borrow to invest?

Well, there are other words for borrowing that investors use like 'gearing' and 'leveraging'. These are very positive words and describe well the effect of borrowing because it levers or gears your investment so that you get better returns. By the same token, if you get it wrong it can accelerate your path to bankruptcy should your investments fail.

Most successful investors will borrow at some point. Obviously the younger you are the more of this kind of risk you can carry. It's not the borrowing itself that is the problem but the decisions you make about your investments that count. Gearing or leveraging your investment simply makes the wheels spin faster in whichever direction you have chosen. You'll either increase your gains if you made good decisions or magnify your losses if you made poor ones.

Borrowing allows you to buy more investments. If you get it right, you own all of the income from the investment and all of the capital gain after you have repaid the loan, and you get the income and the capital gain using someone else's money (see 'The arithmetic of gearing' on page 104).

Perhaps it's because most of us are used to the idea of a mortgage that we are more likely to borrow to invest in property than anything else. However, it makes as much sense to borrow to buy shares. Borrowing to invest in shares may have left a bad taste with any of you that remember how many people lost money when the sharemarket dived in 1987. The market had become extremely hyped, just about everyone was dabbling in the sharemarket and there was a feeling about that you couldn't lose. In other words, many investors had lost their heads and forgotten that the basic principles still applied. Buying shares in largely worthless businesses was the problem. Borrowing only magnified the losses but that was a secondary problem. And it has all happened before, most notably in 1929, and it will all happen again. However, the lesson that should be learnt is to buy quality rather than avoid gearing. It's like the story about the hen that mistakenly sits on a hot stove. She'll never sit on a hot stove again, but she'll never sit on a cold one either!

Whenever you invest in property or shares it is worth considering borrowing. Think of this as a two-step process:

1 Should I buy this investment?
2 Should I gear it?

Splitting the decision helps you to manage any tendency to automatically borrow or, just as unthinkingly, automatically dismiss gearing. You could argue that if you have done your homework properly and the investment is sound, then there is a very good argument for gearing; after all, if you are really *really* worried about gearing, maybe you should also be really *really* worried about your choice of investment? But there are always other considerations: your personal circumstances may not suit gearing, or your financial position may be unsuitable. Furthermore, if the investment is volatile you may not be able to manage the temporary losses or may need to provide some cash from other sources.

Marlene is one of my most impressive clients. She has a portfolio of over thirty properties. She started with very little and has done all of this through borrowing. It goes without saying that she is an astute purchaser of property. She looks at many properties each week and has her real estate agents running around on her behalf. As soon as the first properties showed some growth she refinanced and took the extra money to put deposits on more. She is ruthless in the best sense of the word, totally unsentimental about the properties. Those that don't perform get sold. She can find much better uses for the money. She never berates herself for a mistake, just learns the lesson and moves on. Marlene is now

> a very wealthy woman, and all owing to her hard work and her astute use of gearing. She could never have created this portfolio without borrowing.

Suffice it to say that you should always consider gearing. Don't be tempted to dismiss it out of hand: research shows that many women investors err on the side of being too cautious, and lack of gearing is one of the ways this is demonstrated.

Obviously, you should never borrow to buy interest-bearing deposits because the returns are too low and are also taxable. You would have to pay more (a higher interest rate) for the money you borrowed to invest in these than they would pay you! You can do this unwittingly as well: many of you may have money in the bank earning very ordinary rates of interest and at the same time be borrowers from the bank (e.g. for a mortgage) at a much higher rate of interest. That does not make financial sense.

It is important to learn to be a smart borrower, both so that you can gear your investments as you gain competence and confidence, but also so that you manage any borrowings that you have to get the best deals and to repay the debt in the most advantageous way. Because of the sums involved when you borrow for property, even the smallest differences in interest rate and the time you take to pay off the debt can make thousands (even hundreds of thousands) of dollars difference to your costs.

Gearing is smart but make sure you learn to do it smartly.

The arithmetic of gearing

Imagine that you had $50000 to invest and you decided to buy a little cabin by the beach. You were unwilling to borrow anything so found a really cheap old shack and paid cash. Property values increased over the following year and by the end of it your shack is worth 10% more. If you were to sell you'd get an additional $5000. The arithmetic looks like this:

Investment return

Investment	$50 000
Deposit	Nil
Borrowed	Nil
Growth	$5000
RETURN ON YOUR INVESTMENT	**10%**

If you had chosen to buy a much more expensive property at $250000 you might have used your $50000 as a deposit and borrowed the $200 000. Assuming that you got the same level of growth, the property would be worth an additional $25 000 at the end of the year. Because you had only $50 000 of your own money invested, this represents a 50% return on your investment as shown below.

Gear for wealth

Investment cost	$250 000
Deposit	$50 000
Borrowed	$200 000
Growth (10%)	$25 000
RETURN ON YOUR INVESTMENT	**50%**

Notes – 1 You have to pay for the cost of the borrowings.
2 If the investment falls in value, your losses are also geared.

This shows the power of gearing: it amplifies your returns. Of course, if the property had fallen in value your losses would also have been multiplied.

The example above illustrates the effect on your capital gain. But of course gearing works just as well for income. You can use gearing to own an entire portfolio of property (or shares) and collect all of the income (rentals or dividends) from the other people's money that you borrowed as well as gathering the capital gains.

It's the return on your money that matters!

We have used the concept of return on investment several times so far. There is a further refinement called the internal rate of return (irr). The irr is the return that you receive on your money after all costs, such as the costs of paying interest on any borrowings. So your irr is greatly affected by any borrowings, whether the investment goes well or badly.

You can calculate the irr by taking the total profit on an investment (income plus any capital gain), subtracting any expenses (interest, fees, tax) to get your net profit and then dividing by the amount of your money that was invested at the start:

$$\text{irr} = \frac{\text{net profit} \times 100}{\text{your cash invested}}$$

For example, if you invested \$100 000 and it grew to \$150 000 over a few years (after you had paid your costs) your irr is 50% on your money:

$$\text{irr} = \frac{\$50\,000 \times 100}{\$100\,000} = 50\%$$

If you had geared, and had borrowed an additional $100000 to buy $200000 of investment and it had grown to $300000, your profit would be $100000 and your irr would be 100%:

$$\text{irr} = \frac{\$100\,000 \times 100}{\$100\,000} = 100\%$$

You have an irr of 100% on your money. The irr formula allows you to measure your net return on your own cash.

Time matters

Time matters in several ways when investing: first you have the conundrum of when to invest, then you have to decide how long you will stay in your investment. You also have to consider all of your personal time horizons, such as how old you are, how many years your investment income will have to cover, and at what time you are likely to need your investment money.

Obviously some of these will be connected to each other, but let's think about them separately to begin with.

Timing

When should you invest? The issue here is timing the market. Is now a good time? Will next month or next year be better? Should you buy those shares today or wait until tomorrow . . . or the next day? It goes without saying that you would like to buy when the market is low (so you buy cheaply) and sell when the market is high (sell at the top for a good profit). But it is very difficult to know where the market is for anything. You can always check where the prices have been, but it is extremely difficult to establish where the market is headed next. And the more it looks like it's headed in one direction, the more likely it is that there will be a 'correction', which is the technical way of saying that it will head back towards the average.

It's very easy to become paralysed by this or get reckless! However, the rational approach is to accept that no one knows for certain what the markets will do, and to stop trying to perfect your market timing. Let's assume that you had a lump sum to invest—you may have received a bonus at work or an inheritance, sold the business or farm, or had a property settlement from a relationship break-up. Should you invest it all right now? You may feel you just want to get on with the investment. It's sitting in the bank and everyone is telling you that you are stupid to leave it there because you could earn more by investing it. No doubt someone who stands to make some money from your decision is urging you to buy whatever they are selling. For various reasons, you may also be 'uncomfortable' with this amount of money—you are still hurting from the relationship breakdown, still grieving for the person who left you the money, or indeed grieving for the business or farm you have sold that you put so much of your life into. And you may feel that you did not 'earn' this money and you may be tempted to get rid of it as quickly as possible. Slow down. You never know what is going to happen to the market tomorrow. The more money there is, the more you should slow down the process and take your time. In addition, there's nothing wrong with money in the bank—it's earning 7% as I write, which is a respectable return, and it's safe. If you invested it all today and the market dropped could you handle the losses in the shorter term, given that if it is well spread around you can be reasonably certain that it will come right in the longer term? Don't invest it all today if you can't handle shorter term losses.

You could delay. For example, markets are fairly high at the time of writing. Shares are selling at very high P:E ratios and property seems fully priced: in other words, it's hard to see that returns will rise much for some time and they may well fall. But no one knows and even the professional forecasters and institutional investors do not know. Maybe the markets will continue to rise for a few more years and if you delay you'll miss out on all this growth. Professionals largely avoid trying to time the market; they know they can't. You could wisely make an exception for boom times like the one we are in because we know that they don't last. However, I have now been saying that for a couple of years as the markets have continued to rise! And at other times markets are low—property prices have plateaued or even dropped and the sharemarkets are in the doldrums. These periods usually follow a boom. So you can certainly choose in a general sense better times to buy and better times to sell. For example, it is not sensible to buy lots of shares when most are trading at historically high P:E ratios because the likelihood is that these will come back down to historical averages. The technical term for this is reverting to the mean. If quality shares which historically have had P:E ratios of 12–15 are trading at 15+ you can expect that a shift back to the mean (average) is not too far away. The same is true with property. If good rental property has traditionally yielded about 6% in the area and is now selling on yields of 4% it is selling at very high prices and you could expect a correction. You might choose to keep your investment money cashed up and wait for the sales and some good buying when the market drops. What you should try to avoid is attempting to be very precise in your timing. Only one purchaser can buy at the very bottom and only one seller can sell at the very top—you want to be in the area rather than trying to identify that day, hour or second when the market turns.

The sensible approach is to drip feed money into the market over time. So you take your lump sum and divide it into, say, four, five or six parts and you choose to invest a portion each month or each quarter. This allows you to get an average return while smoothing out the timing decision. The technical term for this is 'dollar-cost averaging'. You average out the dollar cost of what you have to pay for your investments by buying them at different prices on different dates. See 'Dollar-cost averaging (DCA)' on page 118.

Time in the market

You can't afford to be out of the market because of the way it works. If you jump in and out, behaving emotionally and erratically, you risk not being there on the days that the money is made. The markets tend to soar, or dip, on certain days rather than evenly. If you are not there on those days your returns are severely affected. You could, of course, argue that it would be good to miss the bad days too; however, both are entirely unpredictable. Remember what an emotional beast the market is. You need to be there on the days that the beast smiles, and the only way to do that is to be there all the time. This is particularly true of the sharemarket. Most of the gains in the market happen on a few (unpredictable) days of the year. Even property investors cannot afford to be out of the market for long. Who knows what will happen to prices while they wait?

The length of time you are in the market will account for the greater part of your returns. And, of course, the longer you are there the less significant will be your precise timing of when you enter or exit. Time in the market allows you to benefit from the generally upward trend of markets—businesses and property becomes more valuable over time and the long-term averages are all in your favour. Staying in the market for long periods allows you to ride out the blips as well and it allows you to choose good times to sell, when the markets are high for your particular investment. The market adage is that time *in* the market is more important than *timing* the market.

Time in the markets is important because of the power of compounding. Everybody knows that the returns you get on your investment (dividends, rentals, interest, profits and even your capital gains) can earn you even more money if you reinvest them. So, as well as your principal amount of investment earning interest, you can have your interest earning interest by reinvesting it rather than taking it out for consumption. What is surprising is how few people grasp how powerful this effect is if you give it time to work. It seems to give you only a minor additional return in the short term but the effect accelerates. This has a really profound effect on the total amount of your investment after a number of years.

Have a closer look at how this works, because it's one of the most important things that you can learn about money.

Let's say you have $1000 to invest and can get a rate of 10% p.a. If you invest your $1000 you will get $100 interest. You can spend the interest ($100) and invest the $1000 the following year and get another $100 dollars, which you can spend as you choose. This is called 'simple' interest as it is obviously simple—you continue to have the same amount of capital ($1000), you continue to invest it at the rate you can get (10% here), and you earn a sum of interest ($100), which you take and do with whatever you wish. At the end of ten years you have your capital ($1000) and you have also earned ten lots of $100, another $1000.

It looks like this:

Year	Capital	Interest rate	Interest earned	Interest spent	Total at year end
1	$1000	10%	$100	$100	$1000
2	$1000	10%	$100	$100	$1000
3	$1000	10%	$100	$100	$1000
4	$1000	10%	$100	$100	$1000
5	$1000	10%	$100	$100	$1000
6	$1000	10%	$100	$100	$1000
7	$1000	10%	$100	$100	$1000
8	$1000	10%	$100	$100	$1000
9	$1000	10%	$100	$100	$1000
10	$1000	10%	$100	$100	$1000

Now, look at the difference if you *compound* the interest, i.e. add the interest earned each year back into the capital sum and reinvest the new amount.

Year	Capital	Interest rate	Interest earned	Interest reinvested	Total at year end
1	$1000.00	10%	$100	$100	$1100.00
2	$1100.00	10%	$110	$110	$1210.00
3	$1210.00	10%	$121.00	$121.00	$1331.00
4	$1331.00	10%	$133.10	$133.10	$1464.10
5	$1464.10	10%	$146.40	$146.40	$1610.50
6	$1610.50	10%	$161.00	$161.00	$1771.50
7	$1771.50	10%	$177.20	$177.20	$1948.70
8	$1948.70	10%	$194.90	$194.90	$2143.60
9	$2143.60	10%	$214.40	$214.40	$2358.00
10	$2358.00	10%	$235.80	$235.80	$2593.80

What is the difference between simple and compound interest? What is it that means one investor has $2593.80 while the other has only the original $1000? The answer is that one has taken out the interest each year and spent it. The other has left the interest in the system and let it compound so that there is interest earned on the interest. If you think this is an insignificant amount try the example with an investment of several thousand dollars.

The above example is very simple for the sake of clarity. The time period is short and so does not show the almost 'magical' effect of compounding. Look what happens to these numbers if you continue this investment for a longer period:

Year	Capital	Interest rate	Interest earned	Interest reinvested	Total at year end
1	$1000	10%	$100	$100	$1100.00
2	$1100.00	10%	$110	$110	$1210.00
3	$1210.00	10%	$121.00	$121.00	$1331.00
10	$2358.00	10%	$236.00	$236.00	$2594.00
20	$6116.00	10%	$612.00	$612.00	$6728.00
30	$15863.00	10%	$1586.00	$1586.00	$17 449.00
40	$41114.00	10%	$4114.00	$4114.00	**$45 258.00**

The person who invested $1000 originally and took the interest each year ($4000 in total) still only has an investment of $1000 forty years later. She took her $100 interest each year ($4000 in total) and spent it. The woman who left her $1000 to compound now has $45 258! Note especially how the compounding effect is magnified in the later years—it grew over $10 000 between year twenty and year thirty, and over $27 000 between year thirty and year forty. I have to say it again: time is the investor's best friend! Put another way, starting early is the most controllable strategy for an investor.

Jane and Mary are both forty years old. They both start thinking about investing to retire in twenty years time when they will be sixty. Neither of them feels that she has a great deal of money to invest. Jane decides to start immediately and she invests $1000 a month for the next 20 years. Mary decides to wait until money is a little easier to come by in her household. She waits until she is fifty when she is able to invest $2000 a month. In total, they both invest $240 000. Now, let's assume they both get a 7% return. The difference in what they each have at age sixty, however, is significant: Jane's money has compounded to $520 000, whereas Mary has $346 000, a difference of more than $160 000. It is the extra years of compounding that has made the difference.

It's hard to catch up!

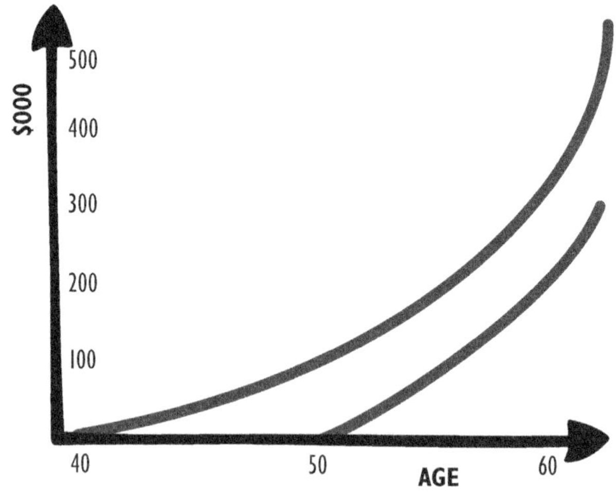

In other words, it is very hard to make up for lost time. Even if you feel that you can spare little now, you are almost certainly better to begin investing as soon as possible. Over a forty-year working life you have 480 months in which to invest. Every one you miss is a waste! You have to invest a lot of additional money later to make up for the lost time. So don't waste energy regretting what you (and I) should have done at twenty or twenty-five, just make sure you don't regret in the future what you should do today.

The Rule of 72

Wealth grows over time. As well as time, the other key variable here is the rate of return/rate of interest. There is a neat 'rule of thumb' to allow you to calculate this. It is called the Rule of 72.

The rule of 72 lets you work out how long it will take for your investment to double. If you know the annual return you can work this out in the following manner.

If you get a 6% return, your investment will double in twelve years: 72/6 = 12. But if you get a 12% return, your investment would double in six years: 72/12 = 6.

So, your investment will double in 72/the rate of interest you receive; or, for your investment to double in X number of years you will need to divide 72 by X to get your rate of return. This assumes that you reinvest your returns and allow them to compound.

You can also use the Rule of 72 to look at the effects

of inflation on your investments: your money will halve in 72/rate of inflation. For example, if inflation is at 3%, your money will halve in 72/3 = 24 years; if it rises to 4%, your money will halve in 72/4 = 18 years.

Dollar-cost averaging (DCA)

People are always concerned about the timing of making investments or converting money from one currency to another—should I do it now or will the rates or prices be better in six months' time? Well, no one can really answer that question with any certainty. The solution is to dollar-cost average.

The concept of dollar-cost averaging (DCA) is about drip feeding money into the market over a period of time, regardless of what is happening in the market or the particular price of the assets you are buying. This money could be a regular contribution, for example, you might commit to make a monthly payment of $100 into an investment or you might have a lump sum, e.g. $50 000, that you feed into the market over six or twelve months. Depending on the price of what you are buying, you will get a different amount of the units or shares each month. The idea of DCA is that you will average out the price that you are paying. Otherwise, you will have to bet it all on getting the right price on the right day and that is very difficult. Dollar-cost averaging removes the short-term timing issues and spreads your risk of buying on the wrong day, i.e. when the market is high. If prices are high, your contribution will buy fewer units or shares in that month; if prices are low, you will be able to get more for your money. Over the period you buy you will get an average price. Dollar-cost averaging is a sound idea. It is what people have always done when they contribute regularly to a superannuation fund.

Let's say you have $100 a month to buy investments in a fund. Each month that amount buys a different number of units, as below:

Month	$Price	Number of units	$Spend
1	$2.00	50	$100
2	$2.50	40	$100
3	$3.00	33	$100
4	$4.00	25	$100
5	$4.00	25	$100
	Average price per unit: **$2.89**	Total units: **173**	Total spend: **$500**

Over a five-month period the price of the units has moved around a lot. You have continued to contribute $100 each month, and each month that has bought you a different number of units. At the end of five months, you have spent $500. It has bought 173 units in total, which means you have paid an average price of $2.89 per unit.

Graphically dollar-cost averaging looks like this:

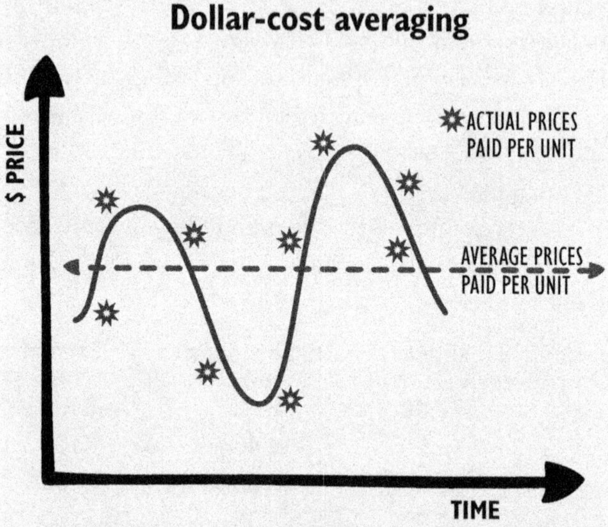

Dollar-cost averaging allows you to stop worrying about when to put money in the market or when to change currencies, and allows you to average out some of the fluctuations.

Superannuation

Ann started work at twenty. She put $100 a month into a super scheme for her retirement every month for fifteen years until she left to have her first baby at thirty-five. She stopped paying into her scheme but could not withdraw the money as it was locked in.

Ann's friend, Susan, began work at the same time. Susan did not feel it was worth saving as she never intended to be in the work force for long; she knew she wanted to marry and raise a family and felt that joining a super scheme was a waste of money. She did marry and have children and feels she has a very successful family life. When the youngest child started school, Susan returned to the work force at the age of thirty-five. She joined the super scheme and has been contributing $200 a month for the last fifteen years.

Ann and Susan are now fifty. Who has the most money in the savings scheme? Surprisingly, Ann has $68 700 while Susan (who has been saving twice as much per month) has $49 000, almost $20 000 *less*.

This example highlights two very important aspects of investing in superannuation:

1 starting early
2 the benefits of 'locking up' the money.

The earlier you begin, the longer your money has to compound. Over long periods of time the compounding effect works very well. When your money is allowed to compound, and when the interest earned is reinvested, even relatively small sums of money can grow to very significant amounts. Remember that Ann made contributions of $100 per month for fifteen years, a total of $18 000. Because it has been left to compound over a thirty-year period, it is now worth almost $70 000. The biggest gains will be in the later years because of the way the arithmetic works. The compounding effect looks like this:

Compounding effect

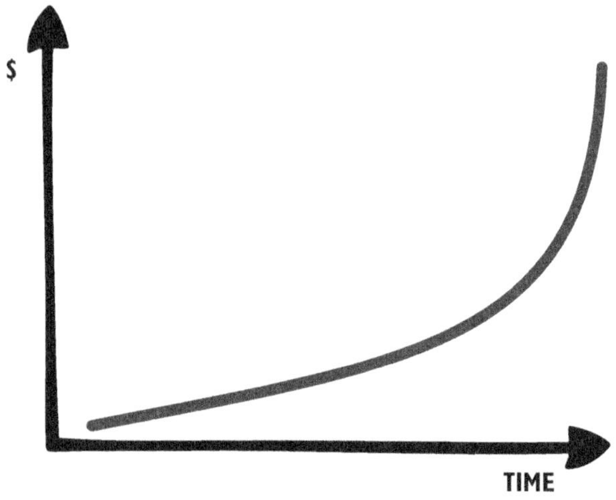

Which brings me to the second point: the benefit of having your savings locked in. If Ann has simply saved through a term deposit account she would no doubt have had many occasions on which she would have withdrawn the money—to pay off the mortgage, to build an extension, to take holidays. One of the very real benefits of many super schemes is that your money is locked up for a number of years and is removed from temptation's way. As such, superannuation can be an excellent means of enforced savings. It works brilliantly for those who struggle with the discipline of making regular savings. It is a form of paying yourself first (see 'Or simply pay yourself first', page 43). If you have difficulty saving then you should look for a form of superannuation that is locked up and unable to be touched.

Different jurisdictions take differing approaches to superannuation. It is compulsory in Australia, for example, while New Zealand has recently introduced an optional scheme. Australian employers are required to contribute 9% of the employee's earnings while the New Zealand scheme will begin with matched contributions of only 1%, rising to 4% over the next few years. However, the basic principles of superannuation still need to be understood whether it is compulsory or not. It is most important that you choose a scheme that is suited to your age and circumstances. When you are enrolled in schemes, you should also monitor your fund's performance carefully and be prepared to switch. It is very important not to make a choice and simply forget about it, assuming that all will be right.

Superannuation can give you a better return for your investment because of two things:

1 tax incentives
2 employer contributions.

Tax incentives

Different countries have different rules and you need to check out what applies in your jurisdiction. However, superannuation schemes are often treated preferentially for tax purposes, with contributions taxed at a much lower rate or with taxation deferred until you make withdrawals. Take advantage of any tax incentives as lower tax rates will enhance your investment returns. Fees often make superannuation funds less attractive than direct investment, but tax incentives can more than compensate for that.

Employer contributions

Many employers choose to match contributions to a superannuation scheme. In other words, they will contribute a dollar for each dollar that you put into the scheme. This is usually capped at a certain percentage of salary, say 5%. You can contribute more of your salary if you wish, but the maximum the employer will contribute is 5% of your pay. From your point of view, this is free money. If you contribute, you can get up to a 5% salary increase. The only catch is that it has to go to savings. If you can avail of such a scheme in your workplace then you should maximise your contributions. If anyone else offered you a free dollar for any dollar you saved, you would bite their hand off!

Even where employers do not offer matching dollars they may offer to pay the fees for the superannuation scheme. From your point of view this is also a valuable contribution, and one you should take advantage of. With the employer paying the costs of the scheme your returns are enhanced because no fees are being paid from your contribution.

Choosing a superannuation scheme

There are a huge number of superannuation schemes to choose from. It goes without saying that it is best to choose a reputable provider. You should also look at the track record of the scheme. While it is no guarantee of future performance, it is an indicator.

Read the marketing material carefully to check for fees. Fees are very competitive in this area but will still vary from scheme to scheme. Above all, you should choose a scheme and provider that suits your circumstances: younger people, for example, should choose schemes that invest in high-growth assets. Some schemes may allow you to pay off your mortgage, which might be very attractive to some women.

A super scheme, whether it is one provided by your workplace or any other one, should be scrutinised just as you would any other investment. Like any other investment or saving decision you make, you need to find out as much as you can about your company's super scheme (or any other scheme you are considering) before deciding whether it's the best option for you. Some of the questions you should ask include:

1. Is there a minimum contribution I have to make each pay period or per annum?
2. Does my employer contribute? How much? Does it depend on how much I contribute?
3. Are there any tax advantages?
4. Who pays the expenses of the scheme? What are they?
5. Is there a vesting period before I can claim the money the employer contributes?
6. Do I have to pay any fees? What are they, and how much?
7. Can I put my contributions on hold (e.g. for maternity leave)?
8. What happens to my savings if I leave the company (in one year, five years, ten years)?
9. Are insurance offers (life, disability, medical) included?
10. Are my savings for retirement only or can I get the money for other things such as buying a house?
11. Can I withdraw without leaving the company?
12. Where is the money invested? Who makes those decisions? Can I make my own decisions? Can I change those decisions at any time? Are there any costs in changing?
13. What do I get when I retire (a pension or a lump sum) and is there a choice?
14. What happens to my savings (and any employer contributions) if I die before retirement?

Some companies provide employee share option schemes (ESOP) to assist employees with superannuation. You end up with money invested in your organisation's shares. In other words the fortunes of your scheme are tied to how well the company that employs you does over the coming years. Some organisations see this as a very good way to align employees with the business: your interests are the same as the business's interests and if staff work hard and the business does well then all will benefit. The flaw in the logic is that much can go wrong that is outside the scope of employee efforts: legislation can change, markets can move, the economy can flounder. And the employee who has a fund based on the company's shares carries a *double* risk. If the company fails they lose their job, and their super scheme may be worthless! This is exactly what happened to employees at Enron—they lost their jobs and their savings as well. I think you should avoid schemes that are based on your organisation's shares unless they are very attractive. Even then you should not invest too much in such schemes because this practice contradicts the principle of diversification, i.e. spreading your risks. Each and every investment should be considered on its own merits. If you would not invest in the company you work for because of objective investment criteria (sound business, good prospects, competent management, good profits), then you should not do so just because you work there.

Over the years, I have come across many women who have not joined either their company's or another super scheme because they intended to be in and out of the work force owing to having children. This is also flawed logic. As the example above shows, you are always better off if you begin a saving scheme as early as possible. Your money, any amount, will continue to work for you even if you have to take contribution holidays, or even if you stop contributing altogether. So don't be put off saving and investing just because you expect to be out of the work force for years.

Getting good advice

You are in charge of your investment strategy but you don't have to do it alone. No matter how well you educate yourself or how well organised you are about your investments you will still need expert help from time to time. There are lots of people who can help. If you are committed to making your investments work then you will make sure that you surround yourself with a 'dream team' of professionals who will assist you in making good decisions and will provide good advice.

Unqualified friends and relations, no matter how supportive, will not know all that they need to know to give you good advice about your investments. And no matter how hard you work at learning about investment you will never know everything and will also find it very difficult to be up-to-date in certain areas. Advisers are useful both in the good times and the tough times, and if the going gets tough you certainly want to be able to call in a 'heavyweight' in the right area. The value of a good adviser is that they have heard it all before.

You are likely to need one or more of the following:

- lawyer
- accountant
- financial adviser
- sharebroker

- real estate agent
- tax specialist
- insurance broker.

It is never easy to choose professionals. It can be especially intimidating if you have seldom dealt with these kinds of people before. However, it's all common sense. Just as when you choose a hairdresser or a medical professional, you need to ask around. No sensible woman is going to pick key professionals from the Yellow Pages. Neither does a sensible woman want to meet any of these people for the first time when she's in trouble. You should start as early as possible. You need to build relationships with them so that you are comfortable with them, and so that they are familiar with your circumstances.

Who you need is determined by your unique situation and what you are planning to do with your investments. The more complicated your affairs, and the greater your goals, the more expert advice you will need. If, for example, you have some share investments and earn some dividends, a general accountant will be able to help you file your tax return and minimise your tax liabilities; however, if you are trading in shares or own a portfolio of rental properties, you may need an accountant with more specialised knowledge.

The best way to find good professionals is to ask around, especially people who are active in the same investments as you. Other property investors, for example, should be able to direct you to good real estate agents, valuers, mortgage brokers and accountants who understand property and the tax law that applies. This is where it can be very useful to join investment groups so that you can network with people who are interested in the same investments as you. However, the ultimate responsibility for choosing professionals rests with you. There are two main rules to keep in mind:

- **Good professionals do what's right for you, not what's right for them.** Naturally, your advisers are in business and have to earn a living, but it is you who should come first. That may mean that they have to advise you to do nothing, send your business away or recommend someone else, even though that means they may earn little or nothing. It can also mean that they may have to tell you at times that you are wrong, and risk incurring your wrath or losing your business. Such a professional is a very valuable adviser and is to be treasured.
- **Good professionals advise you rather than sell to you.** One of the problems for many professionals, especially in the area of finance, is that they only get paid if you buy, sell or change something. Their pay is based on commission, or they receive a fee for the transaction. This is why it is very important for you to understand how your adviser is paid. So it takes a very professional sharebroker to tell you to wait for a month or two.

So how do you find your key professionals? Obviously they need to have appropriate qualifications and experience, with no criminal convictions or bankruptcies. It helps to deal with established and reputable firms, as you can expect that there will be some supervision and systems for keeping the professionals up-to-date and complying with best practice. Word of mouth is probably still the best way to find the individuals that you can work with, so ask around. Ask particularly about levels of service and how satisfied your contacts are with how they are treated. When you have a shortlist of candidates you should meet with each and ask lots of questions to establish if this professional is right for you. Questions might include:

- What are your qualifications?
- What experience do you have working with people in my situation?
- What is a typical client like?
- What sorts of services do you provide?
- How do you work with your clients?
- How are complaints dealt with?
- What research and support do you have?
- What professional associations do you belong to?
- Does your association have a code of professional conduct?
- Are you affiliated with any other institutions? Are you independent?

And, very importantly:

- How do you get paid?

You need to know whether they are paid by fee or commission. As mentioned previously, if your adviser is paid by commission it is in her interest to sell you something, otherwise she does not get paid. On the other hand, if your professional is paid by fee it will cost you no matter what you decide to do. The upside is that your adviser has no reason to steer you in the direction of anything that is not right for you, so there is no conflict of interest. There is really no right answer about how your adviser is paid, but it is best that you know how they are remunerated before you begin the relationship.

Good advice can be expensive: lawyers and accountants will charge for their time, agents will often take a percentage fee, and financial planners, fund managers and risk advisers are often paid a commission based on what you purchase. One way or another *you* will pay; however, I do not begrudge professionals their fees. Ultimately, you get what you pay for. And it may cost you even more if you receive poor advice or seek no expert opinion at all.

In the final analysis, you will have to trust your own judgement. You need to be comfortable with the people you choose, as you will have to work closely with them and will talk to them about many private matters—your finances, your plans, your hopes for the future, and so on. Take your time and choose with care. But always remember that the adviser is working for you, and that you are paying for the service. If you are not satisfied, get a new adviser. Your investments and your future financial independence are far too important to be compromised by an incompetent or otherwise inadequate adviser.

Winners work with winners. Good people like to work with other good people and a good professional in any field can lead you to others. Ideally, you want to have a team of professionals who will work well together to ensure that your investment strategy is successful and will give you what you want. As the diagram below shows, you need each of your advisers to focus on what is right for your investments, and you also need them to work together to help you achieve your goals.

Team of advisers

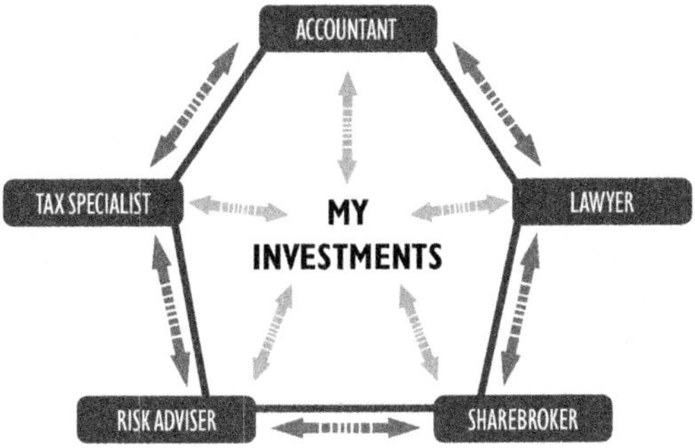

Get the most from your advisers by being prepared and by thinking through what you want from each of them. You will save lots of time (and money) by having all of your information to hand and being organised for each meeting. In addition you should be clear in your brief to the adviser on the following areas:

- What do I want to achieve?
- What advice or help do I need from this adviser?
- Which aspects of my investments will I look after myself and which do I want to delegate?
- What reports and information do I want to receive?
- How much time will I have to spend in this area?
- What do I want to be actively involved in?
- What authority will I give my adviser, and which decisions do I want to make?

Take a sharebroker for instance. Depending on your skill level, the amount of time you are willing to devote to your portfolio, and the level of interest you have in investment, you may make various choices about a broker. You may choose not to use one at all and do all of your own buying and selling online at minimal cost because you watch the market intently and research what is happening in your areas of interest. On the other hand, without a broker you will be unable to access many new listings or investments that the brokers have access to. You will also miss out on the research reports and advice that a broker can offer. You may have neither the skill nor the interest to be actively involved in your portfolio at all. In that case you might give your broker authority to buy and sell on your behalf, operating more like a manager of a fund than solely as a broker. Many of the brokerage firms can also hold custody of your shares, allowing all of your dividends to be consolidated in one statement rather than arriving in dribs and drabs. This makes managing your tax returns simpler and also takes away all the week-to-week banking, filing and administration tasks.

You could choose to have all your dividends reinvested as the broker sees fit or choose to take them as income. How you use the adviser and what her brief will be is your decision.

As with every other aspect of your investments, you can delegate much of the work and decision making but the ultimate responsibility is yours—to choose good advisers, to give them an appropriate brief and to manage them well. Smart women will not be intimidated by their advisers and will ensure that they get the best from each one.

PART 4

PLANNING YOUR INVESTMENT STRATEGY

Does gender make a difference? 139
What's the best investment for you? 142
How much risk can you take? 155
How diversified should you be? 158
How much should you have offshore? 162
Should you invest directly or use managed funds? 166
How should you allocate your investments? 169
Making property investment work 174
Making direct share investment work 181
Big stories—not to be missed! 188

Does gender make a difference?

There are no rational reasons why women cannot invest in any areas they wish. You no longer need your father's or husband's permission to handle your own money. In fact, there is quite a body of legislation to assist you in ensuring that you do not experience any discrimination by professionals or institutions. However, your own practices or mind-sets could get in the way. There is a reasonable amount of research that indicates that women are inclined to purchase low-risk investments. There is nothing inherently wrong with low-risk investments, but your circumstances, e.g. your age, may indicate that you need a considerable allocation of growth assets in your portfolio so that you have enough income from your investments in the future.

In addition, you need to be aware that concentrating on low-risk investments means that you miss out on returns that you could have had without necessarily doing anything too 'risky'. Riskier investments give higher returns and this will make a very big difference over longer periods of time. The difference between leaving your money in the bank and investing it in shares or property over a twenty-year period could be huge.

There is evidence that women are inclined to keep money in the bank because they are afraid that the money might disappear or that there may be short-term losses. If this sounds like you, you should read the 'Manage you risk' chapter again (see page 76). Yes, these risks exist but the way to deal with them is not to avoid them altogether but to manage them through appropriate diversification and purchasing quality investments.

As a woman you may feel that you have very good reasons to adopt a very low-risk approach. You may have dependants and you may also have been brought up to be very risk-averse. Do consider, however, if you are being overly cautious when it comes to investment. And concentrate on growing your knowledge and skills. The more you understand the more your confidence will grow.

This can work the other way, of course. The other body of evidence about gender issues in investment suggests that men trade or switch their investments much more often than women—to the detriment of their performance. Women are more likely to buy and hold. Assuming you have made good choices to begin with, holding your investments for long enough usually gives superior returns. Men appear to be more fickle, trading their investments more frequently. Changing your mind like this is expensive, as it costs both to buy and to sell. It would be dangerous to speculate why this happens. Men may be over-confident in their abilities, they may have a bias for action, they may have ego needs to meet, or they may be very vulnerable to tips and gossip about investments. Maybe it's hormones—who knows! But we do know that these practices generally erode returns and are best avoided.

Another area where gender differences show up is in

the use of professional advisers. Men are more comfortable dealing with people they don't know when it comes to their money and investment issues. Perhaps this is because they are more experienced dealing with professionals through their working lives. I have certainly found that women are very wary about whom they trust with their finances. That is both a good and a bad thing: you certainly need to be wary. Many 'professionals' are salespersons in disguise. I have always believed that the definition of a professional is someone who puts the client's interests first, i.e. who does what is right for the client, rather than what works (makes money) for the professional. So your natural wariness may be well placed. But do use this caution in order to suss out good advisers rather than to avoid advisers or professionals altogether. You need some help and your mission is to find the right people rather than to do nothing. By all means talk to friends and family about your investment ideas and decisions but be very careful of acting on advice that may be well-meaning but misinformed.

What's the best investment for you?

It's too easy to worry about where to invest your money and forget to think about what you want and need from your investments. An investment is not a good investment because the purchase price is good value or the returns are likely to be high or the market looks good. It's only a good investment if it is right for you. You need to match your investments to your needs and preferences and circumstances. It's all about you.

This principle makes nonsense of all of the debates over what is the 'best' investment. People argue endlessly over whether property or shares are best, or whether you should hold bonds or bank deposits. The answer is that they all have their place. What you should own and what proportion of each you should have depends on you. And it will keep changing as your circumstances change. So you should be wary of anyone who wants to sell you an investment who is not taking a keen interest in understanding you and your situation thoroughly.

The technical term for how you split your investments between the different types is called asset allocation. This is much more important than the specific investments that you choose, but many beginners get it the wrong way around. Think of it like this: it's a much bigger decision to choose to put 30% of your money in Australian property than to spend weeks choosing the particular property that you purchase or the property fund that you like. Asset allocation is the 'big picture' of your investment and has to take account of everything about you, such as your age, how much income you need, how easily you need to be able to access your money, how long you can wait for the investment to give good returns, etc. Research indicates that most of your results—your success—depends on good asset allocation at the start. So it is worth putting plenty of time into becoming clear about your needs and preferences. You need to be brutally honest about this and you should do this work before you invest a cent.

The things to explore include the following:

Should you invest at all?

You may think that this is a strange question at this stage—after all, I have been extolling the virtues of investment thus far. However, depending on circumstances, some of you may be better off never putting your money into shares, property or bonds, or even starting a savings plan.

If you have debts it does not make sense to be saving or investing. Your debts might be in the form of a mortgage, hire purchase agreements or even credit card debt. And the question you should be asking is whether you should pay off these debts before you begin saving or investing. It's easy: almost all people with debt would be better off discharging it before doing anything else. The reason is simple arithmetic: you are unlikely to get more from your investments after tax than your borrowings are costing you. If you have a mortgage at 8%, you would need to be getting 11% from your investments before tax before you could consider investing rather than paying off the mortgage. Paying off the mortgage carries no risk, whereas you will have to take a bit of risk to get an 11% return.

Your investment plan should start the moment you have paid off your debt. The smart thing to do is to continue to make at least the same commitment. For example, continue to invest the same amount each month as you are committing to debt repayment.

Repaying debt first will be the smartest financial strategy for almost all women. A few of you may be exceptions to that rule:

- **Are you a skilled investor?** You may be skilled enough to get an after tax return that is better than the mortgage rate.
- **Have you an employer subsidised superannuation scheme?** In some schemes the employer matches your contribution dollar for dollar. That's effectively free money and you would be crazy not to take advantage of it.
- **Are you a direct investor in property?** The combined returns from rental and capital gain (and the possible tax advantages) may mean it's worth investing in property even while you still have a mortgage. But there are risks attached to gearing to buy property and you do need to be skilled at managing your investment.

When you are ready to begin investing there are several other questions that you need to address before you decide where to put your money.

How much income do you need?

Some investments give only income (e.g. deposits) and some give largely capital growth with very little income. This is because many businesses will reinvest most of the profits and pay out very small, if any, dividends. The investments that give high capital growth usually give low income and vice versa. It doesn't matter from an overall return point of view but it may matter practically to you.

Some of you, for example, will be earning high salaries and paying tax at the top rate. The last thing you need is more income that will be heavily taxed. Others will have stopped work and may want some supplementary income from your investments and so might choose to invest in bonds or shares that pay out high dividends.

Fiona is married and her husband owns his own business. He devotes all of his time to the business and reinvests most of the profits. The business has done well to date and it gives them a good lifestyle. Fiona is nervous (and rightly so) that all of their wealth is tied up in the business, so she wants to get some investments outside their company. Her husband is uninterested but is willing for her to take the initiative. Fiona and Kevin will not need any income from the investments in the short or medium term as the business is providing plenty for consumption.

When will you need your money?

Your time horizons really matter. You may want to access this money in the shorter term (less than three years) or you may be able to wait for decades. If you invest money in order to build a deposit to buy a house in a few years time, or to go on a world trip, you need to hold it in cash deposits. You need to be sure that the money will be there, that it will not have lost its value, and you can time the deposits to mature for when you need the money. If you put this money into property or shares, you might be forced to sell them at a poor time and might even lose a lot of your money; you need to be prepared to leave these kinds of investments for much longer so that you can sell at a time of your choosing.

Many funds and unit trusts also charge high up-front fees. Paying these only makes sense if you spread the costs over several years. If you have to withdraw your money early you pay all of the costs but may have accrued none of the benefits.

So think carefully about what amount of your money you need access to in the short term (one to three years) and what can be invested for longer (three to ten years). Bonds and other fixed interest investments will give you a better return than cash deposits at the bank for only slightly more risk. If you can leave your money for a decade or more you will get the best returns from property and shares. Without being able to leave your investment for that length of time you risk having to sell the shares or property at a bad time—the markets are down, the business isn't doing well or it's an election year. Because these investments are cyclical you could even lose money if you had to sell quickly. You are probably wondering why you'd bother given all these problems, but over the longer term you get the best returns from shares and property. In addition, they give you some protection against inflation because they are growth assets and tend to rise in value in line with inflation.

Again, this question of time horizon suggests splitting your money across different types of investment and avoiding silly stuff like putting your savings for a car in the sharemarket, when it should be in a bank deposit timed to mature when you expect to buy the car. It would be equally silly for a thirty-year-old woman to save for her retirement using deposits. She has decades to wait and would get far better returns out of property or shares. The greater risk that's attached to investing in property or shares is lessened by the amount of time. The young woman will see several cycles in the market in that time and has ample opportunity to sell at a time when the markets are high.

Fiona and Kevin have just turned fifty. Kevin's health is good and as the business is almost his hobby as well as his work he has no intention of leaving it any time in the near future. They should not need to touch their investment money for ten to fifteen years.

How much risk can you live with?

This is a tricky question, especially for women. It's tricky because 'risk' means several different things when you are talking about investment. It's a very emotive word in itself. We immediately think of activities like bungy jumping or of pain and hurt! Women are inclined to describe themselves as 'risk averse', sensibly so when it comes to managing their health, minding their children and so on. However, when it comes to your investments you need to consider how much risk you can afford to take with your money.

Age clearly matters: if you are older you can afford less risk as you do not have lots of time to recover your money if you suffer a loss. If you are young you can afford to have nearly all of your investments in growth assets, giving higher returns even though these are riskier in the shorter term.

Your financial position matters too. The more money you have the more you can afford to take higher risks with some of it. You won't end up as a bag lady if some investment goes sour. If you haven't got much you will need to be more careful.

There is an emotional side, too, insofar as it is very important that you are happy and can pass the sleep test—i.e. you are able to sleep at night without worrying unduly about your investments. Too much fear is also bad for your judgement and worried people can do very silly things with their investments. So too can people who are bored—too little risk is not good for you or your investments.

The important thing is to start thinking about your circumstances and your personality preferences. You can always work on changing your attitude (as well as your investment choices), but you do need to know where you are starting from.

> Fiona's desire to have some investments outside the business is a risk management strategy in itself. Business is risky—all business is risky, even successful ones. But Fiona and her husband can still afford to take some risk with their investments and buy some growth assets because they have some time and they have other wealth in the business. However, given that this investment strategy is about lowering their risk they should choose a diversified portfolio of fairly secure assets, a mix of shares, property and deposits.

How much do you know about investment?

In many ways, this is linked to the last question about risk. The less you know about anything the riskier it is. So you may find yourself able to take more risk as your knowledge and skills grow. Watch out too for feeling very brave simply because you have no idea about what you are getting into!

You may feel that you know little or nothing about investment now. That's unlikely to be true; you will know a lot more than you think. Like nearly all other fields of knowledge, it's mostly vocabulary—jargon in other words. It's worth setting out to learn this jargon so you don't feel intimidated.

You don't need wonderful mathematical skills to invest—you learnt all you need to know in primary school. At most, it's basic arithmetic: adding, subtracting, multiplication and division. You'll mostly work in percentages as they allow you to compare things easily. Most of the useful stuff is presented in pictures or graphs.

You do need to know enough so that you are able to ask the right questions and not be intimidated by professionals. The more knowledgeable you are the more you are likely to enjoy investment and be in control of the situation. The more active or hands-on you wish to be, e.g. an active property investor, the more you will need to know. If you do not want that level of activity or detail you can, for example, invest in property through shares or unit trusts.

Don't be too modest in this area: you will be able to learn anything you want to about investment. Remember, it's only jargon.

Investment is ultimately personal. The principles of investment apply to all investment but each of you will need different things from your investment strategy. When you are ready to begin investing there are several other questions that you need to address before you decide where to put your money.

> Fiona doesn't work in the business but has always been an active partner insofar as she has known what is happening at work, discusses the business and people decisions Kevin needs to make and attends the meetings with their lawyer and accountant. So Fiona is not scared of investment. That's what they have been doing all of their married life even if they did not call it that. She knows she needs to bone-up on some new stuff but she's not scared of that and has already started reading about investment in general.

How active do you want to be?

Again, this question is linked to the last. Some investment is much more time consuming than others. If you want to actively manage your property portfolio, viewing houses, dealing with valuers and real estate agents, finding and managing tenants, organising repairs and maintenance, it will take quite a bit of time as well as skill. The same is true for shares—reading reports, talking to brokers, analysing annual reports, learning about industries, keeping up with world events—though the activities are different. Even if you are planning to buy and hold for years, you can't go to sleep on either your properties or shares. There is quite a lot of administrative work to do as well: filing, accounting, banking, tax, etc.

So you need to think about what will work for you and how large a part you want to play in the management of your investments. You can pay other people to do almost everything for you if you haven't the time or don't want to be an active investor. Spending your time as an active investor can be counterproductive depending on your circumstances. If you are well paid it may be far better to devote your time and skills to creating more surplus to invest than to doing the work that a fund manager, broker or property manager can do easily and well.

You may enjoy active investment, however. Some of you will see it as a welcome relief from other responsibilities or as a new and challenging hobby. Be careful not to 'mess in the middle': either commit the time to do it properly or get someone else to do it. Your investments deserve to be well managed.

Fiona has plenty of time to apply to investment. In fact, she has found she is not so busy now that the last teen has gone off to study. She could get more involved in the business but would rather do something on her own. She hasn't decided yet about which aspects she might manage actively. Houses and gardens have always appealed, so she's interested in property and she's used to dealing with lots of people. On the other hand, the bit she has read about the sharemarket is fascinating and she's an old hand at reading company accounts and asking questions of the accountants. In the end she chose a specific area to get actively involved in and will get further diversification in her portfolio through managed funds.

Suit yourself!

	Deposits	Property	Shares
Income	high	med	med
Capital growth	low	high	high
Time for return	fast (1 day +)	slow (5 years +)	med (1 year +)
Risk/volatility	low	med	high
Time involved	low	high	med
Arithmetic skills	low	med	high
Tax efficiency	low	high	med

The three investment classes differ in several ways. You can use the table above to choose what works best for you. Unless you are a very active investor, working hard on your share or property portfolio, you are likely to have a mix of investments in order to get what you want from your portfolio. You might, for example, hold some property and low-dividend shares for growth and to hedge against inflation but have a considerable portion of your money in bonds because you need regular income. Some of your deposits might be at the bank because you travel a lot and want access to some of your money without having to sell any other investments.

How much risk can you take?

All investment is risky to some degree because it means that you have to give your money to someone else, and there's always a chance you won't get it back. We have looked at the elements of managing risk in Part 3. Your greatest risk is the risk of performance, that your investment is lost entirely, or just 'flat-lines' and goes nowhere. The risk of volatility, that your investment is up and down, matters much less the longer you can leave your money in the market. If you cannot afford to leave your money in the market for a substantial period, then you need to make sure that you don't end up with volatile investments that you might have to sell when the market is down.

Performance risk and volatility risk are real and objective. More personal, though no less real, are aspects of your personality that you should factor in. If you are a habitual worrier or are likely to stay awake at night, fretting about your investments, then it is unwise to have risky investments. But do try to be sure that you don't merely accept a bad habit of assuming that all risks are the same, and that the only correct approach is to take no risk. From a financial point of view that's a very risky strategy—the risk of no returns at all!

So the questions I'd ask you concerning risk are:

1 **How much wealth do you have?** If you have plenty, especially if some of it is tucked away in relatively safe

investments, such as a family home, you can afford to take some riskier investments. However, if you have very little you can take relatively few risks. Of course, even with very little, especially if you are quite young, you have nothing to lose!

2 **How old are you?** This is often the most sensitive question I ever have to ask someone! However, my assessment is that if you are over 50 you have to take a bit less risk because you have relatively little time for your finances to recover if you lose your money.

3 **Do you own a business?** Business is risky and if you already have this amount of risky investment, I would recommend that the rest of your investments should be in very secure and highly diversified assets.

4 **Where do you get your income?** If your income is insecure, e.g. you have low skills, are liable to be made redundant, or your income can be turned off easily, then you should compensate by choosing investments that are lower risk.

You may find it helpful to give yourself a score and assess where you sit on a risk scale.

If you are:	Points
Over 50	30
A business owner	20
Relatively short of wealth	25
Insecure about your income	15
Nervous and worry a lot	10
Total	**100**

Now, put yourself on the risk meter:

Risk meter

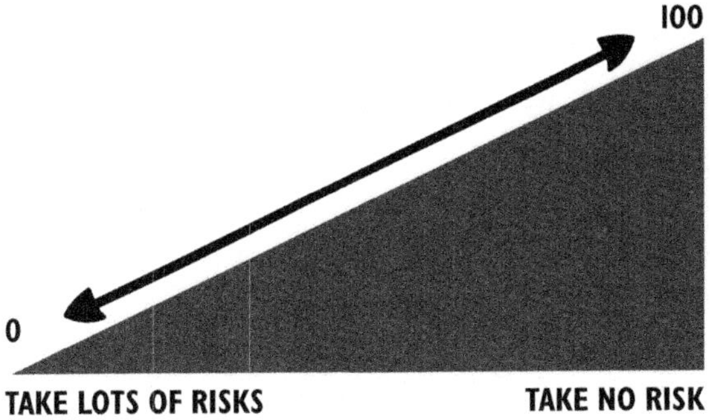

Note that there is no way of deciding *absolutely* and with scientific precision what level of risk you should take. You can weight (give more or fewer points to) any of the areas above differently, or there may be other factors that you think apply to you that are not listed above. But you do need to decide how much risk you are willing to accept. This will greatly affect your investment choices and therefore your returns. The higher you score in the areas above, the less risk you should take, instead choosing lower-risk investments and holding a widely diversified portfolio.

How diversified should you be?

Diversification (see page 86) is about managing risk by spreading your investments in different asset classes so that you are not overexposed to the risks of any one of them. The different investment classes often move in different directions, e.g. bonds are likely to do well when shares are doing poorly, and so diversification helps to maintain your returns overall. Diversification helps you hedge your bets because some investments are countercyclical, e.g. when interest rates fall, share values often rise, because money moves into the sharemarket and out of deposits.

And that's just the asset classes. Within each asset class you have lots of other options to diversify, for example, you can split your money between domestic and offshore investments; and you can choose between investments you hold directly and those held through managed funds. And you can keep going. For example, you can choose between funds that track the market by buying a set proportion of each share on some particular index (passive) and those where the fund managers actively intervene, choosing to buy and sell what they believe will improve performance. This is where investment can start to look complex, but it is not if you approach it methodically.

Some women will have a tendency to under-diversify,

keeping a large proportion of their wealth in relatively few investments, like one or two local rental properties or a few pet shares. On the other hand some may go overboard and over-diversify, which will lower returns and create administrative overload. Diversification is the best way to manage risk—Peter Bernstein, author of one of the all-time best finance books, *Against the Gods*, said that diversification is the nearest thing that an investor gets to a free lunch!

So how do you decide? The questions I would ask you include:

1 **When will you need this money?** Some of you may need income for consumption from your investments soon, while others may not need income for a decade or even several decades. If you do not need the money for a long time then you are more likely to diversify widely to protect yourself against all the things that could happen over the coming years. Similarly, if you are investing so that you can buy a car or have a world trip, you should not consider diversification at all because you should have this money in a cash deposit at the bank.
2 **Where did you come on the risk meter?** If you scored highly (should take less risk), then you should diversify more.
3 **How skilled an investor are you?** The greater your skill the less you need to diversify, as you can back your judgement and expertise more.
4 **How much time do you have for investment?** The more time you have to monitor and manage your investments, the less diversified you need to be. On the other

hand, if you are merely going to keep an eye on your portfolio you should be widely diversified.

You may find it helpful to give yourself a score and assess where you sit on a diversification scale.

If you are:	Points
Investing for the longer term	30
Trying to lower risk	30
Relatively unskilled at investment	20
Going to give investment little time	20
Total	**100**

Put yourself on the diversification meter:

Diversification meter

Note that a higher score means you should have more diversification. What each woman should choose will depend on what assets she already has and also on her investment preferences. But if you scored eighty or more you probably should hold all asset classes (shares, property, interest-bearing deposits and short-term cash deposits), and have some of them offshore. And you should also be diversified within classes, for example, holding several different shares (more than ten and preferably fifteen to twenty), holding property in a variety of locations (easiest to get through property funds, and a range of them too), and holding a range of managed funds.

How much should you have offshore?

Keeping all of your assets in the country where you live is too risky. The smaller the country you are in, the riskier this is, because it takes less to adversely affect that economy. Often single events, like a bad storm or something that affects a single industry, like agriculture or tourism (e.g. bird flu), has a huge effect on the economy overall and on the markets in particular. It's not just about managing the downside either: so much of the investment opportunity in the world is far from New Zealand and Australia. The really big stories in investment at the moment and probably for years to come are in Asia—China and India in particular but also the smaller economies like Korea, Malaysia and Indonesia. Similarly some of best growth industries of recent times that rest on the latest discoveries in science and technology are poorly represented in this part of the world, for example the biggest pharmaceutical businesses are in Europe and the US.

So, concentrating your investments locally is unwise for two reasons:

1 you are overexposed to domestic conditions
2 you miss out on some of the world's best investments.

But there are other things to consider as well. One is the currency risk. If you have offshore investments you are exposed to a profit or loss simply because of the shift in the dollar. You may also want to think of offshore investments to protect the value of your dollars, especially if you travel or hope to travel a lot. If our dollar loses value in the coming years, then travel would get more expensive for us. Holding offshore investments helps you hedge that bet. The other factor to consider is how well you think your domestic economy will do in the coming years. New Zealand and Australia are small players by world standards and you have to be very optimistic to expect them to outperform bigger and more diverse economies elsewhere. If the local economies don't perform well then your domestic investments will neither thrive nor keep pace with growth overseas.

So my questions to you would include:

- **How much do you intend to travel overseas?** The more you are away, the more of your money should be offshore.
- **Where do you expect to go overseas?** You may need investments denominated in a range of currencies.
- **Will you be spending or sending much money overseas (perhaps because of family living overseas)?** You will need more overseas if you are spending a lot overseas, for example, on children's education or supporting other family members.
- **Do you do much business overseas or import goods from a particular area?** Overseas investments would hedge your business activities well.

You may find it helpful to give yourself a score and assess where you sit on an offshore investment scale.

If you are:	Points
Intending to travel overseas a lot	20
Importing or doing business overseas	20
Planning to help family overseas	20
Expecting the global economy to outperform the domestic one	20
Have good knowledge of or contacts in overseas economies	20
Total	**100**

Put yourself on the offshore investment meter:

Offshore investment meter

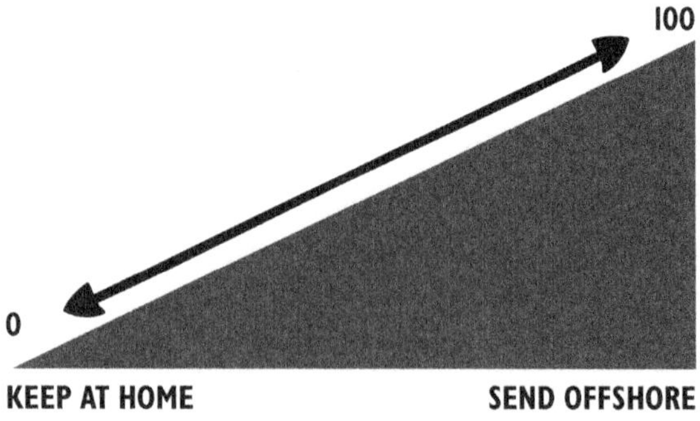

Note you should almost certainly have some of your assets offshore (say 20-30%). Remember also that this is not difficult. If you already have some managed funds you will probably find that a considerable proportion of that holding is invested overseas—check it out. Funds that have a high proportion of overseas investments will be the easiest way for you to get offshore exposure in your portfolio. You can of course purchase shares or property directly, but it obviously takes quite a bit of work. In addition you will have to watch out that nothing takes you by surprise when operating directly in an overseas environment.

Should you invest directly or use managed funds?

It depends. If you invest directly you will have direct control and you won't have to pay management fees either. On the other hand, professional managers have skills that you don't have.

Direct management also takes a lot of time and you should value your time properly—if you could be earning more money to invest that might well be a better use of your time. Similarly, unless you enjoy managing your investments directly, you may be better off paying someone else to do it. But I think the best reasons for using managed funds include access to markets that would be very difficult for you to invest in otherwise. This includes some of the big stories of the age, such as China, and areas like commercial properties which are beyond the reach of the average investor. Managed funds also give you an easy way to meet your needs for diversification—almost by definition they will be diversified in some or several respects.

There is a further advantage to managed funds, especially if you are a woman investing for the first time and have relatively little money. It's very hard to buy much with a few hundred dollars, and fees would make any purchase unattractive anyway. But many funds will allow you to invest small and regular amounts of money, e.g. you can take your surplus each month of $100 and transfer it directly to a fund.

Fund managers are usually well informed, operate within strict guidelines and are well disciplined—all good news for you as it usually means that your money is relatively safe, the fund itself will have spread its risks well through diversification, and the money is being managed 365 days a year.

You could well put all your investment money in funds and use them to cover all of the asset classes. Or if you are skilled or want to have more hands-on involvement, you could still use funds to get your diversification offshore and your exposure to commercial property.

You may find it helpful to give yourself a score and assess where you sit on a managed funds scale.

If you are:	Points
Intending to manage your own investments	25
Skilled at investment	25
Prepared to do the research required	15
Already well diversified	15
Able to take an amount of risk	10
Able to make lump-sum investments rather than drip feed	5
Able to give your investments enough time and attention	5
Total	**100**

Put yourself on the managed funds meter:

Managed funds meter

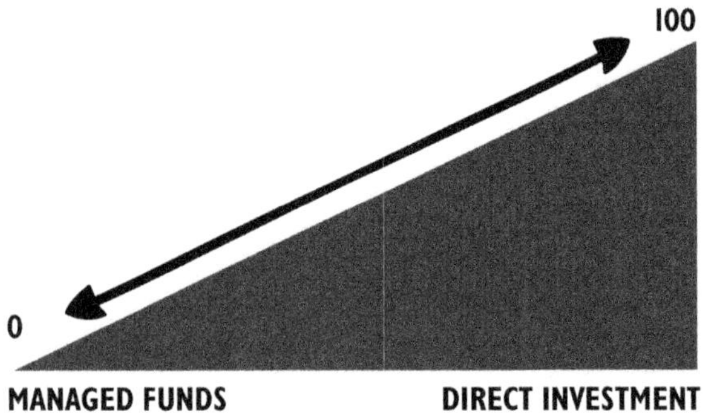

Note that the higher your score the more you should lean towards direct investment and away from managed funds. Be careful not to exclude them entirely—there is almost certainly a place for some managed funds in your portfolio.

How should you allocate your investments?

You have to choose how to allocate your investment money between shares, property, interest-bearing deposits and shorter term ones. There is some science in this decision: research shows that most of your return will be dependent on how you allocate your money. Investment houses can build a portfolio and predict what kind of return you can expect from that mix (allocation) of assets and also predict the volatility of the portfolio, for example, that you will have losses one year out of eight. All of this predictive science is based on what *has* happened so far. So, of course, it only works to the degree that the next so many years will be similar to the last period.

So what should you choose? I would recommend that you take a pragmatic approach. For example, if you do not have a lot of money to invest, then you might very sensibly decide that most of your investment money will go into a few managed funds and you will keep, say, 10–15% in shorter term deposits so that you have fairly easy access to that money.

Jan was left a legacy of $50 000 when her godmother died. Until then she had no investments and found the whole field daunting. Jan knew that this wonderful gift was unlikely to ever be repeated and she was very nervous about making a mistake with the money. As a complete novice and full-time nurse, she did not feel that she could take a very active role in investment. With a teenager, shift work and no partner, she was already stretched. However after a lot of talking and a little reading, her interest was piqued and she decided to try investing. Her asset allocation looked like this:

Jan's asset allocation

Jan put 10% aside to keep in term deposits at the bank. This would provide a buffer that had been lacking and would give a nice feeling of security. She chose to keep about the same amount aside to buy a few shares, using this opportunity as a way to learn a bit more about investment by reading the annual reports, doing a little research, and beginning to take more interest in the business news. The rest—almost $40000—was allocated to four managed funds chosen to give her a good diversification offshore and across asset classes. We decided to buy into those funds over a six-month period in order to dollar-cost average the price she paid. Jan felt that this gave her enough security and involvement, and was the best use of the money for her age (forty-six) and circumstances. She was so pleased with her new investment status that she resolved to set up an automatic payment to herself each month in order to create more surplus for adding to her investments.

How you allocate your money into various investments will determine most of the return on your portfolio so it's important to give it plenty of consideration. Remember that in order to get higher returns, you will need some investments in shares and property. You can offset some of the risk attached to this by having some investments in bonds and deposits. The more shares you have, the more volatile your returns will be. The more bonds and deposits you add, the lower your volatility and the lower your returns. It is estimated that over 90% of your returns are determined by the asset classes you choose so this is very important. It is all too easy to spend your energy on the 'sexy' bits, like choosing which shares to buy or which property or fund to invest in, but it's actually far more important that you get the right balance of asset classes to suit your circumstances.

You will need to reallocate from time to time, depending on your changing needs or changes in the market. Your shares might have done so well that you now own more shares and need to rebalance. However, you do not want to do this too often because you will have to pay transaction costs—the costs of buying and the costs of selling—for each change.

The right asset allocation for you will depend on what you need (income versus growth) and want (what the money is intended for; what you are interested in) and what's required to give you enough diversification in order to manage your risks. Many of you may want to have more active involvement in your investments or may want to build a position as an active property investor or as an active investor in shares. How involved do you want to be?

You may really enjoy the prospect of becoming an active investor. Maybe you have good skills and would enjoy the stimulation of learning what you need to know about your investments. Or you may simply wish to be assured that your investments have been well chosen and are well managed, but you do not want any more involvement than is necessary. Remember that it is the investor that is passive here, not the investment!

Either choice is perfectly fine. You can be as active as you wish. You may choose to invest directly in property, choosing and managing the properties yourself. Similarly with shares: you may enjoy learning about the market, following particular sectors, reading company reports and talking with professionals and other investors.

You can still hold investments in property and shares, or both, without much involvement at all. You can choose to buy an index of shares or invest through managed funds. You might invest a great deal in the property market but do so through shares in a property trust. There is a way to invest in almost anything you want to be involved in and you can choose how great your involvement will be.

But do decide what you wish to do. It is a mistake to choose active involvement if you do not wish to put in the work or will be distracted with your paid work. You may wish to be away for several months of the year. That is no problem with modern communications, but as an active investor you will need to commit to stay in touch with your investments—markets can move very fast.

You will need some professional help whatever you decide. The professionals you will build relationships with will vary with your choices, but you will need to consider the services of an accountant, lawyer, financial planner, brokers and various agents. And whatever you choose you will need to think about how you will manage the people who are working on your behalf. They ought to do the very best job for you, but in the end it is *your* money and it's too important to be left to chance.

Making property investment work

Many of you may see property investment as a great way to build your own superannuation fund. Many women instinctively think of property investment when they are planning to invest. This is because there are many examples of becoming extremely wealthy through property.

However, although it is certainly still possible to become rich by investing in property, it is not as easy as it once was. Property investment used to be the lazy way to riches. With high inflation and low interest rates you could buy just about anything and do well. The only impediment to becoming wealthy through property investment was the amount of money that you could borrow.

The game was to borrow as much as possible (frequently as much as 100%), buy as much property as possible, and wait. Within a few years, inflation would have increased the value of the property, allowing you to borrow more money to buy yet more property. After a decade or two of this, you would have a substantial property portfolio, and great riches. To be successful required little analysis, a simple strategy and no particular expertise or knowledge of the markets. It required neither hard work nor homework, and was a game that could be played (and won) by just about everyone.

Times have changed. It is simply not as easy as it once was—it is no longer the lazy way to riches. Now you do need to analyse, be well informed and go into property in a professional manner. An average performance is no longer good enough; it will not give you enough return. Rather, you have to put in the work to be better than average, to get a return that will be sufficient to make you financially free. You also need to remember that property investment alone can be quite limiting because:

- It is almost always done exclusively in residential property. That means you miss out on the better returns from industrial and commercial property.
- Many property investors end up undiversified with little room in the portfolio for shares, bonds or offshore investments.
- Because property investors are likely to have high borrowings the bank often wants a say in your investment strategy, so you may lose a lot of your independence.

Nonetheless, women are still attracted to property as an investment in part because there are so many examples of women who have done well from it. Women are also attracted to property because of the many books and seminars on the topic, and the heavy promotion of property by real estate agents. In reality, there are some good reasons why property is an attractive way to get rich:

- Property is easy to borrow against. You can buy property and become rich on other people's money (a bank's).

This allows women to make a start with very little of their own money, and if they get things right they can keep on borrowing against the increase in value that they get.

- Property gives two returns: income from rents, and capital growth. While the capital growth side of this is unlikely to be as high as it was, it is still likely to be considerable for those who buy well. Better, along with the capital growth, there is likely to be growth in the income as well, which over time improves the total returns.
- Property is not a particularly volatile investment—its value does not fluctuate widely. As such it is relatively safe (although not, of course, without risk).
- Property investors play with big numbers. A relatively small percentage increase in value can be a significant increase in the investor's net worth.
- There are bargains in the property markets. Property markets are not perfectly efficient, and there are often properties that can be bought well below their true value.
- Properties can be enhanced to increase their value well beyond what is spent on them.
- Property investment is the dealmaker's dream. Those with good negotiating skills can use them to their advantage when dealing with vendors, purchasers, tenants and financiers.

Everyone should have some investment in property, as it's a good hedge against inflation. It can give high capital growth with little income or high income with little growth. If you think you might live overseas at some point then some offshore property holdings should be considered essential. You can hold offshore property investments through a managed fund, syndicate or listed company. You can hold them directly, but make sure that you understand the different legal issues that may apply and that you have good overseas advisers.

Property investors are in constant debate with investors in shares about which is better. The answer is neither. Both give good returns; both have their place in a sensible investor's portfolio. The respective values of each never get too far apart, because the money in the market moves as investors climb into whichever is offering the better returns at that time. As prices go up, returns go down and the money moves.

There are very real risks in having most or all of your investments tied up in property, so be careful that you do not become infatuated with property and end up with a skewed portfolio. It is the same asset class as your home (likely to account for most of the rest of your wealth) so you can end up completely undiversified. Property is a real tie if you manage it yourself and you will be constantly on call—tenants and maintenance issues can be very time consuming, and this may not be the most productive use of your time. If you delegate the management, you will have to give away some of your returns in fees. Property is relatively illiquid—you often can't sell it as quickly as you want and you can't easily sell down part of a property—so it can be hard to get your money out if you need it in a hurry.

If you are committed to direct property investment you need to learn to do it well. Make a good start by:

- studying the market in your area
- learning about the wider market in your region/country
- reading the many books which are available
- joining a property investors association
- viewing lots of properties
- meeting lots of real estate agents
- learning how to calculate the key numbers
- learning how to evaluate a rental property
- trying to identify below value properties
- learning to negotiate
- learning how to manage tenants
- learning to buy well.

Buying property with your head

More than ever before, your wealth from property is created when you purchase. In days of higher rates of inflation and rapidly increasing property values, time took care of your mistakes—almost any property was a good buy over time. That is no longer true. The first thing you need to understand about buying property is yield. The yield is the annual income from the property as a percentage of the cost. You should base your investment decision largely on yield.

You calculate yield before borrowings because these vary over time. Yield takes no account of capital gain. Much of the property that is currently bought as an 'investment' is bought at too low a yield—buying a second home in the same area is almost always in this category.

To win with property, you need to buy property with a good net yield, which ought to be at least 10%. To do this you will have to seek out 'bargains' or property that is available below its true value. You should aim to buy 10% below value. Buying below value is the easiest way to acquire a good, high-yielding portfolio. Capital gain is an additional bonus. The higher yielding the property is the more it will be worth in the future—remember, income values capital.

It is more difficult to get high returns in the residential property market, as the market has a lot of players and is very busy. This means there are fewer bargains. Those who are serious about becoming wealthy through property often focus on industrial property. Industrial property has higher yields, usually has longer-term leases, generally has good tenants and is easier to manage overall. However, industrial property is not for amateurs. The entry price is higher and it is often harder to exit if you make a mistake. Get it right and it offers superior returns.

Skilled property investors, those who are likely to get rich through property, are always in the market searching for bargains. The property market is not especially efficient and bargains are available. There are always people who have to sell quickly. Again, good contacts and good knowledge of the market are needed if you wish to do better than average; however, it is not difficult to learn how to be successful in property—you only need to be willing to do the homework and the hard work.

The cost of making mistakes in property is high as the property market is expensive to enter and exit. There are many one-off costs associated with property, such as lawyers' and agents' fees, so you want as little 'churn' in your property as possible. It's a long-term investment and you need to plan to hold for several years.

And now for a word about 'investing' in your own home. Many women rationalise that their own home is a great investment. Not so. You do have to live somewhere and it's a very good idea to own your own home as it forces you to save. It also provides hedge against upward movement in the market, which might make renting very expensive or might prevent you from owning a home at any time in the future. However, to keep pouring money into your home while calling it an investment is a mistake: it is not an investment because it is not giving you an income. It may give you good value growth in the future, but you don't know. You also cannot release the wealth in your home until you sell: in other words, you cannot eat a house! Many women have too much house, i.e. far too much of their net worth is tied up in the home, which does not give them any income. You can easily find yourself under 'house arrest' at some time in the future, owning a valuable property but with no cash flow to live on. Most women care very much about their home, but do try to keep wearing a smart investor's hat.

Remember, the money in property is largely made when you purchase. Becoming wealthy from property requires that you get good capital growth. You need to buy the right properties to achieve this.

Making direct share investment work

Many women are a little scared of direct investment in shares. While anyone can, and should, invest in shares through a mutual fund or by buying an index, growing your wealth by direct investment in shares requires a great deal of time and energy invested in understanding markets, industries and individual companies. But it's worth it. Over time, shares give very good returns.

If you choose to directly invest in shares, you will need to invest in a very targeted way. Serious share investors are very different from the average investor in the share market. To achieve the kind of returns that will make you financially free you will need to be:

- **Highly disciplined.** Usually you will have your own rules and guidelines for investing and you will stick to them. These rules would apply to matters like the values you would buy or sell at (P:E ratios; the proportion of your investments held in any particular share).
- **Committed.** To invest for superior returns you will devote a lot of time to watching the markets, managing your portfolio, and educating yourself about what is happening in the industries and companies you are

interested in. You will need to develop good finance and business skills as this is what shares are all about.

- **Tuned in.** You will cultivate a network of well-informed people like stockbrokers, business people, other share traders, industry specialists, etc. You will read widely, study company reports, and attend appropriate meetings and seminars.
- **Objective.** To be highly successful at share investing you need to be able to make rational and logical decisions in the face of all of the emotion that is the sharemarket. You will have little or no emotional attachment to your portfolio. You will buy and sell with your head not your heart.
- **A long-term investor.** Three years is an absolute minimum as anything less can see you caught in an economic downturn. Five to ten years is preferable. Shares are volatile—they go up and down a lot. So you need to arrange your investments so that you are never in a situation of having to sell, but can do so at a time that suits you.
- **Conscious all of your other exposures**. If you own a business or farm you are already highly exposed to the economy you live in. You would be too narrowly diversified if you put all your other money into the domestic sharemarket and would be better diversified if it were invested offshore.

You can buy your shares directly through a broker or online. You will pay more if you use a broker but you will also get more help and advice, including reports and research from the brokerage firm. It has to be said, though, that even when you buy online you are going through a broker—it's the broker's website that you are using, in effect. Even so, fees online are very low, but you are on your own. Whichever way you buy, remember that it is the choices you make when you buy that will determine your success.

When you identify a share you wish to buy you can ask your broker (or check online) what price it is selling at. You can choose how many shares you wish to purchase and the broker will enter your bid to the stock exchange. You will be informed whether your bid was successful. Once that happens you have to pay for the shares within a short period via your broking firm, or immediately online. The whole transaction happens very quickly because the prices are changing all the time. That's why you see some people perpetually watching their computer screen, waiting to see the price at which they are willing to buy or sell. You will receive written confirmation of the transaction. Store this carefully for your records.

So, practically this is all very easy to do. Computers have made it much simpler and faster. The bit that requires more time and scrutiny is researching and planning what to buy.

Choosing shares

Simply put, you are looking to buy shares in a good company, in a good industry and in a good economy. This requires work. You will find that everything that happens in the world is of interest: politics, economic shifts, social change, demographic shifts and technological innovations, even the weather!

To beat the market you will have to buy shares that are outside the mainstream—you have to pick winners. This entails much more risk than simply investing in an index (see below) of shares or buying through a mutual fund (more below). Investing in shares in order to become financially free will mean some or all of the following.

- Buying shares that are not in the index. This is often because the companies are very small. Small companies as a group offer good returns but carry more risk.
- Buying shares in start-up companies. Again, the risks are high but the returns can be very good also.
- Buying shares in only a small number of companies. The lack of diversification raises your risk. However, if you pick the right companies you also outperform the averages.

A skilled investor will have shares in fewer companies, many of which will be smaller. They will often restrict themselves to a few industries and will ensure that they understand these industries and companies very well. If you are seeking average returns only you should do just the opposite. You should have a diversified portfolio, perhaps tracking an index or through a mutual fund. While the skilled investor is taking more risk, that risk is mitigated by the expertise that they have.

Good share investors are largely impervious to the market—they are focussed on the trends in economies, industries and in particular businesses. You will be seeking to buy value and to hold the shares. While you cannot afford to forget about them, you will be unlikely to buy and sell often if you have made good choices. A good discipline is to approach the purchase of any share as if you were buying the entire company. You will seek to know everything you can about the industry and that business in particular. Disciplined investors will seek to satisfy themselves about:

- company performance
- growth in profit
- asset quality
- management acumen
- opportunities
- brands, patents, licences, etc.
- threats
- competition.

Successful investors are seeking value. In short they are looking for companies that will deliver sustained profits. Whether these profits are paid out as dividends or retained is largely immaterial—either you receive income that can be reinvested, or the retained earnings will drive up the share values. Sustainable profits are the key to value investing—your challenge is to determine how likely those profits are and how much you should be willing to pay for a share of them, i.e. what is the P:E or Price to Earnings Ratio. To be successful at choosing specific shares yourself you need to become quite knowledgeable about business in general and the evaluation of individual businesses.

If you find that there is too much work or too much risk involved in being a direct share investor you could try a combination:

- Buying some shares directly yourself.
- Buying shares through managed equity funds. The managers will choose and manage the portfolio. They are trying to outperform the market and will trade actively to do so. Sometimes they do well; other years they lag behind the market.
- Buying some passive funds. These funds will passively trade an index either in your home country or offshore. The fees are low because there is little work to do. The fund will do as well as the market. It will be up if the market is up and down if it's down.

A reasonable plan for women who want most of their investment in shares would be to put the bulk in passive funds in order to get cheap exposure to the sharemarket, to put some money in one or two actively managed funds in the hope of outperforming the market, and to hold a small number of shares directly. Arguably, that gives you the best of all worlds and does not require an undue amount of your time.

Buying an index

Buying an index of shares is a simple way to buy a range of shares without having to do a lot of work. There are many different indexes but think of it as buying the top twenty shares in the market. The index you buy will contain some of all of them in proportion to their value in the market. So, if Vodafone represented 10% of the market value of all of the top twenty shares, your index would contain 10% Vodafone shares. Buying an index is like buying the market. You are looking to track the growth of the market. If the top twenty shares together move up 15% over the next year, the value of your investment will too. You will neither underperform nor overperform the market segment (in this case the top twenty) that you choose.

Buying funds

This is essentially the same idea. Your fund could be made up of shares alone or several asset classes. There are funds for just about everything you might want to buy. It's a great way of getting exposure to a lot of shares in a wide range of industries or across several international markets. You do need to pay attention to what the fund invests in as you may unwittingly have the wrong asset allocation, e.g. you might have invested directly in domestic shares and buy into a fund that has all its share investments in local shares also.

Remember that there is nothing wrong with passive investment in shares. In fact, it's the only way to get exposure to some industries and the only convenient way to invest in overseas markets.

Big stories—not to be missed!

We live in very interesting times. In the last few decades the world has undergone extraordinary changes and developments. In just about every area we have seen huge progress driven by new science discoveries and advances in technology—telecommunications, medicine, pharmaceutical, agriculture, engineering, bio-engineering.

Politically and economically many parts of the world have revamped their mind-sets and started to show great ambition for the future of their people. Just look at Asia: only a few decades ago, Japan was the only significant player. Now we see enormous productivity and growth in China, India, Indonesia and Korea.

This is all incredibly exciting for investors. As a keen history student, I have always thought how exciting it must have been to be an investor during the height of the industrial revolution—the invention of the steam engine, the mechanisation of production through steam and machinery, the possibilities created by the coming of the railways and steamboat engines. I suspect however all that pales into insignificance compared to what is going on around us at the moment. This can seem intimidating because much of it is new. It's very difficult to figure out what to do about emerging technologies or particular emerging economies. And how on earth could you possibly expect to choose a particular business share in which to invest in a Chinese province? Well, you couldn't and you shouldn't—you'd almost certainly get it wrong.

But you should invest in these new big stories. It's hard to understand what is happening as it happens—it's always easier in retrospect. However, it is reasonably clear that the eastern economies are on a roll that won't stop for a long time. They have the will and the human capital. This is what you should invest in.

The way to do this is through funds that target these regions or technologies. You can buy shares in a fund that invests in China and India, for example. You do not have to choose the shares yourself. What you are investing in is the continued growth and productivity gains in these countries. These economies have years of high growth rates to their credit and there is every indication that it will continue for some time.

Big stories to consider include:

- **China.** China is the most populous nation on earth. Political change over the last decade or two has led to great economic growth, and it's rapidly industrialising. With its lower labour costs and its huge will to achieve, China is on a path of growth for decades to come. Much of the world's manufacturing is already moving there. Chinese people are becoming better educated and earning better incomes than ever before—their consumption alone will ensure that this economy will expand rapidly in the foreseeable future.
- **India.** India is on a similar path. Again, political thinking has changed and is leading to rapid growth. Many

Indians are well educated and have good English language skills. This has made India a very attractive place to offshore technology businesses. Its economy is predicted to expand for decades to come as more and more of its people emerge from poverty.

- **Asia, generally.** Other Asian countries, notably Taiwan and Korea, are following the same trends as China and India and are feeding off their spectacular growth. Much low-cost production is moving to Vietnam, for example, as China and India graduate to more sophisticated production.
- **Technology stocks.** We have seen great advances in technology over the last decade or two. We know more and can do more in many areas such as communications, medicine, agriculture, security, banking and so on. Technological change looks like it will continue to affect most sectors.
- **Travel and tourism.** The globe is experiencing an unprecedented level of travel and tourism. Again, despite concerns about terrorism and difficulties owing to greater security precautions, this trend shows little sign of slowing any time soon. Australia and New Zealand are particularly attractive to world travellers.
- **Aged care.** The baby boomers are turning sixty. Life expectancies continue to rise. This is the largest cohort of westerners ever to enter their senior years. Expect to see unprecedented demand for lifestyle options, elective medical procedures and all kinds of products and services that you would expect this age group to need or want.
- **Sustainability.** The threat of climate change is forcing the world to rethink how we create and use energy,

water and other resources. Expect to see plenty of emerging businesses around things like wind energy, water treatment and recycling technologies.

It's too difficult and too risky (unless you have expert information) to pick particular investments in most of these areas. However, it is relatively simple to get exposure to the expected growth in the above sectors. For example, you can buy a managed fund that specialises in global technology stocks or you can invest in commodities like oil, gas, silver and iron ore in the expectation that there will be strong demand for these owing to the industrialisation in China. What changes do you see on the horizon? What investments might you find interesting?

Some time in the future your children or grandchildren will ask, 'Gran, you are a highly successful investor. It sure must have been very exciting to be around at the beginning of the century when all those amazing things were happening. What did *you* invest in?' I don't think you will want to say that you ignored China because you didn't quite know where to start or that you didn't look at the technology sector because it seemed a little intimidating. What's going on in the world is what makes investment interesting; investing is interesting too because it encourages you to take more notice of what's happening around you.

PART 5

TAKING ACTION

Doing what it takes 195

Doing what it takes

Any woman can become an investor; you do have what it takes. I hope by now you have seen that investment is as simple, or complex, as you want it to be. You can choose to spend as much or as little time on investment as suits. Likewise you can opt to become quite an expert or you can choose to be largely a passive investor, tracking the growth of the markets but doing very little other than creating a surplus for investing from your finances.

But you do have to do something! Many of you will have hurdles of one sort or another to overcome so that you can be a successful investor. Some of these hurdles might be very real, such as finding a surplus to invest in the first place, while others might be a matter of removing mental blocks that are holding you back. These barriers are in the mind, but they are no less real for that. Some of you may have to have difficult conversations with partners and children about expenditure, lifestyle and habits. We all tend to shy away from this kind of conflict, but if things are to change with your finances, you need to face up to whatever it is that stops you. The best way to address any problem is to solve it! Many of these 'problems' will disappear once you decide that the future is going to be different.

Making changes

Change is hard. That's why so many of us are stuck. Even if we don't like what we have, it's easier to put up with the way things are than to change them. And changing your spending habits, asking your manager for a raise, or looking for a new job takes a bit of effort. Some of you will also be thinking about the energy (and skill) needed to involve a partner in your efforts, if that's what you wish to do. All of these kinds of 'soft' things are often harder to address than the 'hard' stuff, like learning about P:E ratios, comparing various managed funds and calculating property yields.

One of the keys to making changes, even difficult ones, its to focus on what you want to change. I recommend that you spend a lot of time getting very clear about what you want for the future. Some of that is always about what you most definitely don't want: lack of choice, lack of sufficient resources for essentials, lack of money for some of the things that make life enjoyable, lack of independence, and so on. If you can be very clear about *what* you want and want it enough, it is easier to summon up the energy to figure out *how* to make the changes. If what you want really matters, you'll find it easier to change. This is why having clear dreams and reasons for change are so important—if these are not powerful enough to get you going then you will lack motivation to get started. You need to be able to focus clearly on what you will have, the life you will be able to live, instead of getting stuck worrying about what you might have to let go. You get what you *really* want, not what you ask for. So think about who and what you love: the people and the stuff that really matters. Taking care of your money and your financial future is an act of love: wealth allows you to look after those you love. Your 'meaning plan'—what it's all for—is more important than your financial plan, which is only the way to get the stuff that means the most.

Your 'buts'

Some women get stuck on 'buts'. 'But I don't have any money to start with', 'But I'm too old/too young', 'But my partner won't like it'. Ultimately, you have to just get on with it. Otherwise all you get for keeps are your buts! It's worth thinking about the 'buts' and excuses for inaction that are going through your head. Listen to what you are telling yourself and question whether these beliefs are helping or hindering you in your search for financial freedom. I find that many women carry a lot of mental baggage about money. This can vary from feeling that money is somehow 'not nice' to believing that you have to be 'highly intelligent' to be an investor, or that you need a good 'education' in order to be smart about your money. When you write these beliefs down, they look ridiculous. That's because they are. Any woman who is old enough to read this book and who has enough interest and common sense to pick it up is smart enough to figure out anything she needs to know to get her money sorted. It does pay to write down the things you are thinking and that may be stopping you because it's easier to challenge your thinking and to deal with your feelings when you are aware of them. What you tell yourself is important. Listen to the discs you are playing in your head, and put in a new one if it helps you do what you need to do to start investing. For example, you are not a bad or selfish or greedy person for taking care of your money and learning to be a good investor. In fact, the opposite is the case. It is in everyone's interests (as well as yours) that you are able to take care of yourself for as long as you live, and that you have the resources for an enjoyable life. So don't delay because of any misplaced sensitivities. All this negative self-talk amounts to a pile of baggage about money, investment and achievement. It's not helping you have a good life, rather it's providing a set of excuses for why things are the way they are and why it will always be so. You are smarter than that. Throw out the baggage and get on with getting what you want for yourself and those you care about. Watch your language and be very careful what you tell yourself. After all, these are the most powerful conversations you will ever have.

It's all about behaviour

Many investment books focus heavily on personality. I am nervous about this as it is very easy for personality to become yet another excuse for staying in a rut and having a lot of bad habits. When we believe we do what we do because of our personality we feel stuck: 'I can't change my personality, so I guess I'll behave in this dysfunctional way forever'. Nonsense! Your basic personality does not change but you can choose new behaviours any time. If your habits are keeping you poor then choose some new ones, e.g. saving some money rather than spending everything. Your temperament is not your destiny; you can choose to have new habits that are certain to give you what you want in life. Having said that it is important that you continue to observe and understand yourself. One of the areas that keeps coming up for women is believing that they are risk-averse and, therefore, make conservative investors. Unfortunately, this often translates into choosing very low return investments, even when that is clearly a poor asset allocation for that woman. You can be conservative and risk-averse and still have a portfolio with a suitable amount of growth assets for your circumstances.

Being a successful investor is nearly all about behaviour. It is not about personality. It isn't even much about knowledge, because you can be a very successful passive investor with relatively little knowledge. But it is about behaviour. You have to invest and you have to have the discipline (habits) to create the surplus that allows you to invest. So don't worry about your personality; focus on developing the habits and behaviours you need to get what you want.

Don't procrastinate

One of the most unhelpful behaviours is procrastination, leaving it for another time. My favourite way of helping someone to overcome procrastination is to tell Mark Twain's parable about eating frogs! He says that everyone has 'frogs' they need to eat: conversations they need to have, phone calls they need to make, paper work that needs attention, decisions that need to be made. He says that unsuccessful people get up every day, see these frogs at the breakfast table—and try to ignore them. They know they will eventually have to swallow the frog, but they keep trying to put it off for as long as possible. This is a pointless way to behave as the frog must eventually be eaten. On the other hand, Twain says that successful people get up every day and, far from avoiding frogs, they look around to see which is the biggest one to eat. And they eat it. And then they look for the next most important frog, and the next, and so on. And so their lives progress. They make things happen. It's a good parable.

Taking action—any action, no matter how small—is essential for moving towards your desired results. Our self-esteem withers when we sit around contemplating problems and wondering how to proceed. The only thing that makes you feel effective is to do something. Once you get started it's easy to keep going, but you must begin. So make a phone call to an adviser, join an investment group, set aside a few dollars, or go online and look at some annual reports or listings of shares. As someone once said, 'It's not because things are difficult that we do not do them, it's because we do not do them that things are difficult!'

And don't delay a moment longer. Time really matters to your money. If you leave it you will have to take real risks in order to get the returns you will need. Be smart and waste no time. Be savvy and plan to get wealthy, but slowly. That's the smartest and the safest way to invest.

Now that you know what you need to do, now that you know what difficulties you need to address, make a list of the frogs you need to eat in order to become a successful investor—and then eat them. Doing the difficult stuff is always a winning strategy. But you knew that . . .

Printed in Dunstable, United Kingdom

88180806R00127